*Royalties from the sale of this book
will be donated by the author to community
organizations serving the needs of children.*

Why Am I So DAMN Unhappy?

And what to do about it

James Downton Jr., Ph.D.

a.k.a Bob, the Happiness Coach

Copyright © 2008 by James Downton Jr., Ph.D.

All Rights Reserved.

No part of this book may be reproduced without written permission from the publisher or copyright holders, except for a reviewer who may quote brief passages in a review; nor may any part of this book be reproduced, stored in a retrieval system, or transmitted in any form or by any means electronic, mechanical, photocopying, recording or other, without written permission from the publisher or copyright holders.

Robert D. Reed Publishers
P.O. Box 1992
Bandon, OR 97411
Phone: 541-347-9882; Fax: -9883
E-mail: 4bobreed@msn.com
Website: www.rdrpublishers.com

Editor: Barbara Harrison
Cover Designer: Cleone Lyvonne
Typesetter: Mait Ainsaar, BICN Marketing & Design

ISBN: 978-1-934759-02-8

Library of Congress Control Number: 2007908766

Manufactured, Typeset, and Printed in the United States of America

Important Disclaimer: This book is sold with the understanding that the author, contributors and publisher are not responsible for the results of any action taken on the basis of information in this work, nor for any errors or omissions. The publisher and the author and contributors expressly disclaim all and any liability to any person whether a purchaser of this publication or not, in respect of anything and of the consequences of anything done or omitted to be done by any such person in reliance, whether whole or partial, upon the whole or any part of the contents of this publication.

*For my students, who cared so much about creating happiness that
they were willing to work hard to achieve it.
I'll never forget what you created
and I'll never forget you.*

ACKNOWLEDGMENTS

Many people helped me to improve this book. They include my family, Mary, Katherine, Diana, and Jason, and my students, Amanda, Andre, Blair, Carley, Casis, Erin, Fox, Kelly, Kua'i, Lisa, Sarah, Serena, Seth, and Travis.

Pam and Deb, mothers of two of my students, made important contributions, as did Sara, a staff member in my department.

At Robert D. Reed Publishers, I appreciated Barbara for her expert editorial work, Cleone for her creative sparks and vibrant book cover, and Bob Reed for his sense of humor and inspiring presence.

Thanks to all of you for your honesty, insights, and helpful suggestions to improve the book. What you did made a big difference.

TABLE OF CONTENTS

Dedication	V
Acknowledgments	VII
Introduction	XI
1. The Almost-Ironclad Guarantee	1
2. Being Attacked By "The Punies"	5
3. Prove It!	13
Creative Sidetrack	23
4. Placing Blame Is A Great Game	25
5. Beating Yourself Up With Stories	29
Creative Sidetrack	35
6. Lower The Bar A Few Inches	37

7. There Should Be A Law Against Put-Downs	45
Creative Sidetrack	53
8. Self-Pity Creates Some Great Whining	55
9. Vampires And Angels	63
Creative Sidetrack	71
10. Fears Are Knots Tying Up Your Mind	73
11. Going On Guilt Trips	79
Creative Sidetrack	85
12. Up To Your Eyeballs In Lies	87
13. Feeling Red With Envy	93
Creative Sidetrack	99
14. Resistance Just Makes You More Miserable	101
15. Visiting Your Tombstone	105
Creative Sidetrack	111
16. Finding Your Inner Wisdom	113
17. Putting A New Spin On Your Life	119
Creative Sidetrack	125
18. Meeting The Almighty Coach	127
About The Author	137

INTRODUCTION

This book might be called "self-help fiction" because it features an imaginary character called "Dr. Bob, the Happiness Coach." As the playful and candid part of me, he tells stories about people he coached. Each story highlights an issue that makes people unhappy, and then Bob shows us how to deal with it—sometimes with humor, sometimes with blunt honesty.

Dr. Bob's stories are based on my years of university experience teaching personal development to adults, whose ages ranged from twenty to sixty-five. The stories Bob tells reveal issues my students shared about what made them miserable. I developed the strategies of change that Bob introduces to help people develop more happiness in their lives. I know from experience that the strategies work, although diligent practice is required. Happiness isn't something you find. It's something you create by constantly practicing new ways of thinking and being.

During the writing of the book, Dr. Bob developed a personality of his own, bringing playfulness to the serious issues of personal growth. As a comedian, Bob sometimes surprises me with his off-the-wall humor and imagination. He has famous people appear out of nowhere as coaches, stars like Humphrey Bogart, Katherine Hepburn, and Woody Allen. Behind Bob's wacky and hard-nosed persona, there is compassion and love for the people he coaches because, as he says, "I live mainly for one thing—to help people become happier." As I was writing the book using Bob's voice, I grew to appreciate his playful nature and down-to-earth, no-holds-barred way of helping. I learned to love the guy. I hope you do too. Get ready to meet Dr. Bob!

CHAPTER 1

The Almost-Ironclad Guarantee

"If people worked as hard to achieve happiness as they do trying to lose a few pounds, they would change overnight."
Steve - fitness trainer

Hi, I'm Bob, your happiness coach.

I'm a shade over sixty, have white curly hair, stand quite tall, and have a bit of width and wildness. A few years after graduating from college, I became a stand-up comedian. I was pretty good, so I traveled around the country doing small nightclubs. I loved humor, so it was fun in the beginning. Then the cigarette smoke in the clubs got to me. I never took up smoking because I thought it was stupid. When I read about the health effects of breathing the exhaust of other people's smoking addiction, it woke me up. I quit the club scene in a hurry.

After giving up my comedy career, I drifted from job to

job, not knowing what I wanted to do. Being at loose ends, I started to feel like my life didn't have any meaning. For about a year, I dug myself into a hole of self-doubt and indecision. Feeling lost, I decided to see Sophie, a down-to-earth counselor who combined different trends in psychology and religion. She was in her forties with beautiful black hair and a mysterious, healing spirit. She knew her stuff and set me straight in a hurry.

As I became happier, I recognized how resigned I had become to my unhappy life, as if it were normal. Don't get me wrong. I wasn't completely miserable. I'd say I was like most of my friends—happy some of the time, but unhappy too much of the time. A lot of people live that way, thinking they have about as much happiness as they can get or deserve. Sophie didn't let me settle for that, like the day she put her hands alongside my head, looked me in the eye, and said, "Bob, what you don't reach for, you'll never get, so always be reaching for happiness." I have never forgotten that sweet moment of encouragement, and I've never quit reaching for happiness.

While I was working with Sophie, I went back to college to get a Ph.D. in psychological counseling. I was a counselor for a long time, until I came up with the idea of being a happiness coach. As a happiness coach, I felt freer to confront people about the various ways they made themselves miserable. If people took responsibility for their unhappiness rather than blaming other people or their circumstances, they would become like columns of white light. Well, maybe more like a 100-watt light bulb is closer to the truth, but that's better than living in the dark.

With coaching, you will achieve more happiness in a week. I know you're skeptical. I would be, too. Notice I'm hedging my bet by saying "more" because there has to be a bit of misery left over so your mind has something to do. This makes my guarantee almost ironclad, which isn't too bad.

I intend to make this book small enough so you'll be able

CHAPTER 1 — The Almost-Ironclad Guarantee

to read the whole thing while visiting the john. It may take several trips. However, the book will be so interesting and life-changing that you'll want to spend more time in the john. Can you imagine the conversation you'll have with your mate?

"Honey, would you please quit hanging out in there? I have to brush my teeth."

"I can't help it. I'm working on my happiness."

"I know achieving happiness takes a long time, but this is ridiculous."

"Two more minutes and I think I'll have it."

We should take the task of achieving happiness seriously, but sometimes we get too mentally tight while trying to create it. So, as you prepare to achieve more happiness in a week, be serious about it, but also loosen a few screws in your mind. When your mind is open and flexible, change will come more easily.

I live in a house with playful spirits running around, and sometimes they show up during a session. Apparently, they can't resist wanting to help. This gives my happiness coaching an element of surprise even for me, because sometimes I'm caught off guard by the people who visit—like the time Groucho Marx showed up to help a guy whose life was so messed up that he was thinking about getting a job. I still remember what Groucho said to him. "There's only one thing worse than looking for a job, and that's finding it." Anyway, be prepared for a few surprise visitors.

I live mainly for one thing—to help people become happier. I hope you will become one of those people.

CHAPTER 2

Being Attacked By "The Punies"

*"The world is screwed up because people who feel
little on the inside try to make themselves feel
bigger at someone else's expense."*
Tina, social studies teacher

You know you're in the running for the top unhappiness prize when a hot fudge sundae can't cheer you up. When you're that unhappy, you can buy one of my artistic creations. It's a T-shirt with the following words across the back: "Caution: You're standing behind a deeply, profoundly, excruciatingly miserable person." The front says, "I'm Number One and No One's in Second." The great value of being able to wear this T-shirt is that you get to make other people laugh when you couldn't give birth to a laugh even if you had a C-section.

WHY AM I SO **DAMN** UNHAPPY? James Downton, Jr., Ph.D.

The punies story comes from my time with Wendy. She came to see me because, as she said, "Dwelling on my misery has become almost as time-consuming as watching TV." On the day of her first visit, she wore a sharp-looking white jacket, red blouse, and black pants. She had dark brown hair, light brown eyes, and a funny way of smiling. I could smell the faint aroma of her makeup. I was wearing my downwardly mobile garb: faded jeans, loafers, and a red sweatshirt with one of my inscriptions on it. It said: "Life isn't your biggest problem. Your mind is." I remember Wendy smiled when she read it.

Bob: "Ah, Wendy, I see a spark of light in you."

Wendy: "I do have a few good moments. They call you Dr. Bob, isn't that right?"

Bob: "Some people call me that, but I don't advertise it. "Bob" will work just fine. Wendy, welcome to my abode. I'm glad you've come. I hope you are. Come on back to my study."

Wendy: "I like your house. It looks turn-of-the-century."

Bob: "Yeah. It was built around 1890."

As I led Wendy into the study, we made small talk. Inside, she commented on the large windows, the red couch, and the imposing photograph of Humphrey Bogart behind it. I love being surrounded by famous entertainers. Up on the walls with Bogart are large photos of Katherine Hepburn, Lena Horne, Woody Allen, Jack Nicholson, Sidney Poitier, and Fred Astaire.

Wendy: "You like movie stars, I see."

Bob: "Yeah. They remind me that life is a stage and we're all acting up."

Wendy took a place on the couch while I sank into my favorite green, stuffed chair across from her. She looked nervous.

Bob: "So what do you want to work on?"

Wendy: "I've heard that you help people to become happier and, while I'm not desperate, I can use more happiness

CHAPTER 2 — Being Attacked By "The Punies"

in my life."

Bob: "Well, let's get to the heart of it then. What makes you unhappy?"

Wendy: "Quite a few things."

Bob: "Give me some examples."

Wendy: "Well, sometimes I become unhappy with the way people treat me. Like the other day at work, my boss criticized me for a small error I made in a report without saying anything good about it. My report was excellent, except for that small problem. I felt so unappreciated and stupid that I got depressed afterward."

Bob: "Did you say anything to your boss?"

Wendy: "No. Instead, I was down on myself for making such a stupid mistake. I'm down on myself a lot."

Bob: "What makes you do that?"

Wendy: "Hmm, making stupid mistakes for sure. I also get on my case when I've mistreated someone, like a couple of weeks ago I told a friend that she was being bitchy. I felt terrible about myself afterward because I knew she was just having a bad day. A couple of days ago, when my boss asked me to work extra hours, I lied to her about why I couldn't. For the rest of the day I felt bad, thinking there was something so cowardly about me that I didn't exist as a real person."

Bob: "Sounds like your inner judge is really harsh."

Wendy: "Some days I feel like I'm on trial and my judge has already made up his mind that I'm guilty. He takes over and makes me miserable with his constant criticisms."

Bob: "Would you say that you're living in automatic, like a machine?"

Wendy: "What do you mean?"

Bob: "Most people think they're free, but they react automatically to almost everything without thinking. That's what I mean by living like a machine."

Wendy: "I've never thought of myself as a machine, but I

WHY AM I SO **DAMN** UNHAPPY? — James Downton, Jr., Ph.D.

guess that's the way I react sometimes, like last week when I was down on myself. My judge took over so quickly, I wasn't able to put up any resistance to him."

Bob: "You're not the only one with this problem. Most of us behave like machines. Our feelings of inadequacy force us to live that way. Would you agree that feelings of inadequacy tend to control us?"

Wendy: "I know I feel inadequate too much of the time, especially when I compare myself to people who are confident and together."

Bob: "Do you ever share your feelings of inadequacy?"

Wendy: "Are you kidding? I hide them, even from many of my friends. I don't want them to know I'm a weakling."

Bob: "What do you think your friends do when they're feeling inadequate?"

Wendy: "I'm not sure."

Bob: "Well, I have a secret to tell you. Everyone feels little and inadequate at times. It's the feeling of being a small child who is weak, frightened, and insecure. I know you've heard the expression 'thin skinned.' Well, feeling little on the inside is what creates it. Most people hide how little and inadequate they feel, including guys who come across with the strength and confidence of John Wayne."

Wendy: "That's comforting, if it's true."

Bob: "I'll give you an example from my life. When I was a stand-up comedian, I was at a party after a performance when a half-drunk guy I knew yelled across the room, 'Bob, I like you, but you're not funny!' His comment made me feel so little on the inside that I said something crude and walked out. Ever have times like that, when you reacted without thinking to what someone said or did to you because your ego was deflated? When your ego deflates, what happens?"

Wendy: "Sometimes I strike back if someone has said something to hurt me, like you did at the party. When I'm

CHAPTER 2   Being Attacked By "The Punies"

feeling little, I also become vulnerable to the judge in me who keeps reminding me of my shortcomings. Sometimes I lose confidence, which makes me uncomfortable around people. At other times, I might go to extremes to promote myself, showing off what I know and can do. I can even put other people down to lift myself up. I hate that about me when I do it, especially when I get into spreading negative gossip."

Bob: "If we lived inside other people's minds for one week, we'd be surprised to discover how often they feel little on the inside. This makes them vulnerable to all kinds of thoughts that undermine them. A friend of mine calls this barrage of self-criticisms when our ego is deflated an 'Attack of the Punies.'"

Wendy: "What a funny idea, yet it captures how I feel sometimes. I experience attacks of the punies more than I'd like. I wish they'd leave me alone."

Bob: "What kinds of things bring on puny attacks for you?"

Wendy: "Let's see. I guess I'd say not having the perfect face and body brings on a puny attack sometimes. But I could make a long list of things, like believing that some people don't like or respect me, being rejected by anyone about anything, feeling like I don't fit in, failing to impress people enough, and feeling stupid or incompetent. It's no wonder that I'm not happier. Who could be happy with puny attacks going on all the time? Is there a way out of this?"

Bob: "Well, a puny counterattack is a useful strategy. Since a puny attack comes from our feeling of being little and inadequate, we have to counterattack with our feelings of adequacy. This puts a stop to the automatic nature of our responses so we can make a different choice. Does this make sense?"

Wendy: "I think so, but how do I counterattack when the punies are attacking?"

Bob: "You already have a strategy, although I'll bet

you've never thought about it. When you experience an attack of the punies, do you ever say something to yourself that helps you regain your balance?"

Wendy: "Let me think. Yeah, that happened a few nights ago. I was at a party and a guy I know said, 'Wendy, what the hell have you done to your hair?' This woke up the punies for a direct attack because I felt unattractive and rejected. I struggled with my feelings for a few minutes and then I said to myself, 'Hey, Wendy, you're a good person, so get over it'."

Bob: "That was a great puny counterattack because you were affirming what makes you adequate. You're a good person, no matter what people think of you or your hair."

Wendy: "Yeah, I see what you're getting at. I wonder if there are other statements I can use. What statement do you use?"

Bob: "When I experience an attack of the punies, I mount a counterattack with 'I'm good enough.' What other counterclaims can you use? You can use mine if you want."

Wendy: "You have a good one. I know I'm good enough, at least most of the time. Let's see, what other counterclaims might work?"

Bob: "What about doing this together? You come up with a claim, and then I'll come up with one."

Wendy: "Okay. Here's one that might work. 'This isn't going to kill me.'"

Bob: "'In the big scheme of things, this is nothing.'"

Wendy: "'I know my mom loves me.'"

Bob: "That's a good one. Here's another: 'I'm strong enough to deal with this.' So tell me Wendy, what do these counterclaims do to the punies?"

Wendy: "Well, I know they help put them in their place. Beyond that, I'm not sure."

Bob: "You've got the idea. We give punies power by accepting their negative claims as the truth. In contrast, our

CHAPTER 2 *Being Attacked By "The Punies"*

counterclaims are positive thoughts we use to live in happier and more productive ways. Creating positive thoughts helps put the punies in their place."

Wendy: "This seems like difficult work."

Bob: "It's definitely not easy and, when you're really upset, it might not work at all. But it's a good strategy to use. Being human isn't easy. It takes a lot of effort to be aware so we don't behave like machines, but hard work and patience will increase your chances of achieving more happiness. See the inscription on my shirt? What does it say?"

Wendy: "'Life isn't your biggest problem. Your mind is.' So everything we covered today is about the way I think."

Bob: "Change how you think and you'll change who you are and how you live. The change wouldn't happen overnight. By gradually changing your thinking, you'll see more happiness appear in your life as if by magic. The great part is that you'll be the magic maker."

Wendy: "So my thinking is the problem! Thanks. This has been a good session."

Bob: "For me, too. I'm imagining a new inscription for a shirt. It would read, 'Puny Club of America, open to people with little egos and big judges.'"

Wendy: "I'd buy one. I'd be the first member of the club. I'll bet it would attract a lot of people."

Bob: "Unfortunately, it would probably be millions."

A few days later, Wendy left a message on my answering machine. She told me that she had helped a friend develop a counterattack to the punies. Her friend had come up with the counterclaim, "Instead of taking this personally, I'll learn from it." I love it when people I coach pass along a lesson to a friend because not only does it help the friend, but it also embeds the happiness principle in the person who teaches it.

COACHING TIPS

- Realize that you're a machine. Get out of automatic by exercising your ability to choose. Know that, no matter what the situation, a creative choice is always possible.
- Think positively about yourself to stop your inner critic's tendency to point out your shortcomings. Do this by becoming a manager of your mind. Run your mind, rather than being run by it.
- When you're under a puny attack, counterattack with a positive statement about yourself that affirms your adequacy and goodness.

CHAPTER 3

Prove It!

*"When you quit trying so hard to prove yourself,
you improve yourself."*
Evan, artist

I'm creating a new board game called "Prove It!" The object is for players to rack up as many points as possible to prove that they're special. You roll dice to move your piece around the board. Wherever you land, you have to draw from a deck of cards. Drawing from the deck creates two possibilities: You have proved your value so you can move ahead, or you haven't and have to go back. One of the cards says, "You just gave a talk and stammered so much that you felt like an idiot. Go back two spaces." On the positive side is another card, "Someone at work called you 'a creative force.' Go ahead three spaces." These cards alone will make the players see how hard they try to prove themselves, but the most interesting part of the game will be when they draw a surprise card.

Surprise cards require players to explain what they do to prove that they're special. For example, there's a surprise card that says, "Explain what you do to be right in an argument to prove your superiority." Another says, "Explain how you exercise control over others to prove you're the boss." There are other cards requiring players to explain what they do to prove that they're physically attractive, compassionate, and smarter than a cabbage, things like that. These surprise cards will make people squirm because they'll have to face how hard they try to prove themselves on a day-to-day basis. What is worse is that they'll actually have to admit it.

Trying to prove our value in life is a lot like a board game, in which our goal is to make enough points to justify feeling superior to others or at least to feel good enough about ourselves so we're willing to get out of bed in the morning. The best definition of a human being I've ever read is, "A large bag of water with a brain floating on top." It sounds like an ice cream soda, doesn't it? How can people possibly think that they're better than others if they paused to understand this? So what's the main goal of our effort to prove our value? To be accepted and respected by others so we will feel worthwhile and happy.

Proving our value is so automatic that most of us don't know how much time we spend doing it. I have already mentioned a few ways that people try to prove themselves, like being the boss, being always right, being smart, being attractive, and being compassionate. But there are many other things people want to prove, like they're
>perfect,
>competent,
>smart,
>morally superior,
>cool,

brave,
in control,
independent,
loveable,

and some people try to prove that they're tough and dangerous.

Everyone's pushing hard to prove that they're really something, even though, in the big picture of the universe, it's kind of a joke. We are something, but just not as much something as we'd like to be. I'll bet the Almighty Coach would say, "In the big picture, human beings are small grains of sand in my sandbox. I use them to build castles to amuse myself because I have a lot of time on my hands." Yet, even though we're like grains of sand, we want to always look big, like castles. This makes trying to prove ourselves inevitable, which can make us tense and unhappy in a hurry.

A case in point was Charlie. When I first saw him at my front door, I thought, "This guy looks like an overstuffed couch." His muscles were huge and bulging. He was clearly hoping to convince me that he was macho-attractive and no one to mess around with.

Bob: "You look like you're a weight lifter."

Charlie: "Yeah. It's something I do."

Bob: "I used to have muscles, too, but when I reached sixty, they left town without me."

Making our way into the study, Charlie took a seat on the couch.

Bob: "So what brings you here?"

Charlie: "I need some coaching about a relationship I'm in that's driving me off the edge. I've been seeing this woman, Monique, for about six months. We met through a friend and got serious in a hurry. Overall, the relationship is good, but there are times when she says something that makes me feel like there's something wrong with me. Sure, she says good things, especially about how I look, but she has tricky ways of criticizing me."

Bob: "Give me an example."

Charlie: "Well, the other day she said, 'What if you went to college so you could get a better job?' This felt like a put-down because she has a college degree and I don't. I quit in my sophomore year because I hated going to classes. Right now, I'm working at a machine shop making custom parts for racing cars. I like the work and make a decent living. I think Monique loves me, but I feel insecure around her. When she criticizes me, I wonder if she's getting ready to leave me. This makes me feel so vulnerable that I go out of my way to please her. I also try to convince her that I'm smart and worth having around."

Bob: "Is trying to prove your value something you do mainly with Monique, or is it a general tendency?"

Charlie: "I'm always trying to prove myself. But isn't everyone?"

Bob: "Yeah, we're all in the game, but each of us has unique issues. What are you hoping to prove?"

Charlie: "That I'm smart, a good guy, and easy to be around. Stuff like that."

Bob: "What are you hiding?"

Charlie: "You don't fool around do you? We've just met, and you're going to the heart of it."

Bob: "I'm sorry, but what's the point of hiding? It's part of our problem. Whenever we try to prove our value to other people, we're also trying to hide our weaknesses. It's like two sides of the coin. By looking at what we do to get acceptance and what we hide to avoid rejection, we come to a fuller knowledge of ourselves. See my point?"

Charlie: "Yeah, but I'm not feeling comfortable with this. You know how guys have a hard time expressing their feelings about personal stuff. I feel like I'm going to pay a price if I'm really honest about this."

CHAPTER 3 — Prove It!

Bob: "Well, what do you want to do? We can take this up at our next session."

Charlie: "Yeah. That would give me time to get used to this touchy-feely stuff. I wasn't prepared to reveal my weaknesses right away. I need a bit of time to warm up to it."

I asked Charlie to share some things about his life that he felt comfortable telling me. He described coming from a large family of six kids. He was the youngest. His father was a factory worker at an auto plant, and his mother was a housewife who also worked cleaning houses to make ends meet. Charlie struggled to get through school, and he had one scrape with the law after stealing a car with a friend to take a joy ride. He lived in a tough neighborhood. "That's when I started lifting. I wanted to look big enough so guys would stay off my back." He also talked about his interest in high-performance race cars. He had a fantasy of racing someday but said he hadn't done anything about it.

I also came from a tough part of town so I couldn't help liking the guy. He was a survivor like me, and he was down-to-earth. When our time was up, I turned the conversation back to the issue of hiding because there was something I wanted him to think about.

Bob: "After you explore what you hide, I'd like you to identify the life metaphor you're living in."

Charlie: "What's a life metaphor?"

Bob: "You've heard the expression, 'Life is a bowl of cherries.' Well, that can be a life metaphor. If you lived within that idea, you'd be noticing how abundant life is, which would affect how you think and live. I worked with a guy once who lived in the metaphor that life is a prison. As a result, he felt trapped, controlled, and rebellious. Most people don't know that they live in metaphors and how much they're affected by them. Sometimes people have more than one metaphor, but often there's a guiding one. If they live in a negative metaphor,

WHY AM I SO **DAMN** UNHAPPY?   James Downton, Jr., Ph.D.

it's sure to produce a dose of despair. When they change their negative metaphors to positive ones, they turn an important corner in their lives."

Charlie: "What's your metaphor?"

Bob: "When I was younger, I lived in the metaphor that life is a struggle, so I struggled a lot. Now I live in the metaphor that life is a playground, so I play a lot. You can imagine the change that happened to me when I made that shift."

Charlie: "Yeah, I can see what might happen."

Bob: "Anyway, spend some time thinking about your guiding life metaphor, okay?"

Charlie: "Okay. I'll give it a shot."

We ended the session at that point. People need time to make changes. First they have to take time to understand what's making them unhappy and to figure out what they need to change, and a lot of time bringing the changes into their lives. It's hard work that doesn't produce big results overnight. The slow progress can be disappointing at times.

When I was younger, I became discouraged when I slipped back into some bad habits for a while. It made me feel that I was never going to achieve the kind of happy life I wanted. I told my Aunt Maggie about it. She was my favorite aunt because she combined playfulness and wisdom. She said something like, "Changing isn't easy, but it's much easier than balancing a banana on your nose. Changing yourself might be slow and difficult, but it beats the alternative. Some people never change, so they miss the adventure of life. Don't be one of those people. Be aware enough, smart enough, and bold enough to become happier and more playful as you age. Never join the people who wallow in their suffering as if that's what life is about. Life is not about living in the dark, but bringing light to it. If you give up on change, you give up on the light. Now, why would you want to do that?"

It was two weeks before Charlie came back. I happened

CHAPTER 3 — Prove It!

to be wearing one of my T-shirt creations. The words on the front were, "There's only one thing I fear more than death and that's your rejection." When he saw it, he laughed and said, "You have two of my biggest fears there." Walking behind me toward the study he added, "Okay, let's make a deal." He had read the words on the back. "Let's make a deal! I'll accept you, if you'll accept me."

Bob: "Let's keep the fun going as we talk today. Fun keeps the mind flexible so it will reveal things it never would admit under normal circumstances. If you play around with the issue of what you hide, what would you say?"

Charlie: "Seeing what you're doing, I'd say you're a tricky guy."

Bob: "Yeah, sometimes I sneak up on people hoping they'll wake up without knowing it. You've had a couple of weeks to think about what you hide. What did you learn?"

Charlie: "I'm still feeling awkward about this. Where do I begin? Well, I saw how much I hide my frustration and anger when Monique complains about me. I also hide my lack of confidence because I don't want people to think I'm weak. I hide my fears and feelings so I appear strong and independent. To be honest, I'd have to admit that I hide how vulnerable I feel behind all this body bulk. I think those are the main things."

Bob: "We're all hiding what we think are weaknesses because we're afraid other people will reject us when they find out. So you're like the rest of us. We're all in it together, pretending to be someone else instead of revealing ourselves. What about your life metaphor? Did you work on that?"

Charlie: "Yeah. I was pretty surprised because it came to me so fast. For years, I've been living in the metaphor that life's a competition I have to win."

Bob: "Is that working for you?"

Charlie: "In a way, it does. It makes me work harder at my job so I can get an edge on the other guys at the shop."

WHY AM I SO **DAMN** UNHAPPY?   James Downton, Jr., Ph.D.

Bob: "And what about the down side?"

Charlie: "I see most people as competitors. Hiding my weaknesses and proving my worth are strategies for making points so I can gain an edge in the competitive game."

Bob: "Is there another metaphor that would make you happier?"

Charlie: "Yeah, I thought about that. I tried on different ones and decided that I liked 'life is an adventure' the best."

Bob: "What would that do for you?"

Charlie: "Well, I wouldn't be competing with other people all the time. In fact, they could join me in the adventure. We could work together. I think I'd also be more willing to take risks because I wouldn't be pushing so hard to impress people. I'd probably have a lot more fun. Maybe I'd even take up racing cars."

Charlie began to laugh.

Bob: "What's up?"

Charlie: "I'm seeing how being human is a tough job. Instead of thinking that's bad, I can see it as part of the adventure."

Bob: "I just finished reading a book about near-death experiences. There's a story in it about a woman whose heart quit beating during an operation. Moving toward her death, she went to a place where there were beings of light. One of them told her that she wasn't ready to pass through the barrier because there was still something she needed to finish on the physical plane. As she began to leave, another being of light said to her, 'Tell everyone you see that we appreciate what they are doing to evolve because we know it's hard to be a human.'"

Charlie: "That's great! It makes me wonder what the next step should be for me. What do you think?"

Bob: "It's your life, so it's really up to you. Wait, I just remembered a letter I have that might help. I'll get it."

When I returned with the letter, I told Charlie, "A woman

CHAPTER 3 — Prove It!

I worked with a couple of years ago wrote a letter to her favorite uncle, asking what he would tell people about how to live so they'd be happier. This is a copy of the letter the uncle sent back. He said,

'Become so interesting that you enjoy being in your own company. Instead of worrying about fitting in, put your energy into seeing how far you can develop in your lifetime. You are the most important work of art there is. Create a self that makes you unique, happy, contented, and fulfilled.'"

Charlie: "That letter makes a good point."

Bob: "It's also in line with living your life as an adventure. Now, you can create yourself as a work of art. That should make your adventure more interesting."

This session helped Charlie turn his life around. By living in the metaphor that life is an adventure, he became less cautious about hiding his weaknesses and bolder in the way he expressed himself. Instead of holding back his feelings, he told Monique how he felt when she slipped in her subtle criticisms. She welcomed the change because it meant that they could work more openly on their relationship to improve it. She eventually accepted the fact that he wasn't interested in going back to college.

As for Charlie's inner life, he worked harder to accept and respect himself so he wasn't as driven to seek the approval of others all the time. He became a stronger person on the inside, not just on the outside. When I spoke to him a couple of years later, he was still working on the change. "I've learned that change takes time," he said. "Time's going to pass anyway, so I might as well keep at it." I remember thinking, "Charlie's one smart guy."

Now that you're aware of the pitfalls of trying too hard to prove yourself, I have to tell you about another card in the game "Prove It!" It's the "Super Surprise Card." It says: "Explain how you make other people in your life prove their value to you. What do they have to believe and how do they have to behave for you to accept them? How does what you require make them unhappy? Seeing what you're doing, what changes will you make?" This card is the most eye opening of all because, while it's fairly easy to see how other people put pressure on us to prove our worth, it's harder to see how we pressure others to bend to our wishes. "Prove It!" goes both ways.

COACHING TIPS

- Instead of trying so hard to prove yourself, learn to accept and like yourself. Become a good friend to yourself as a step toward being a good friend to others.
- Become aware of your guiding life metaphor. If it brings you down, then use a new metaphor to raise yourself up.
- Become so interesting that you enjoy being in your own company. When you do, you'll like yourself better, and others will want to spend more time with you.
- If you put pressure on people to prove their worth to you, think about the misery you create for them and how you might change what you're doing.

Creative Sidetrack

Time to refresh! What are the first five words that come to mind when you think about your personal qualities? Your leading qualities can be negative as well as positive. You may be too controlling, but also kind. Be honest.

Now that you have your attributes in mind, look to see whether "creative" is among them. If it isn't, add it to who you say you are. Identity is largely fiction anyway, so revise your personal story to make "creative" one of the first things you say about yourself. What will happen when you live in the belief that you're creative and can ask at any time, "What's a creative way of relating to this problem?"

Take a minute to think about creative ways of approaching an issue that's making you unhappy.

How does taking a creative approach help you solve the problem so you can be happier?

A poster hanging in an office of a friend says it all. "Are you in a rut? Be a revolutionary. Think creatively!"

CHAPTER 4

Placing Blame Is A Great Game

*"I love blaming others to avoid looking at me.
This makes for a great day 'cause I don't get depressed
about what I won't allow myself to see."*
Johnny, poet and songwriter

Imagine a game show on television called *Place the Blame*. On the game show, contestants get to blame someone in their lives for making them unhappy. To make the show interesting, contestants make true and false claims to four judges. If the judges catch a contestant in a lie, the contestant loses five points. The contestant wins five points for every lie the judges accept as true.

The winner of a game gets to bring the person blamed onto the show. That person is given a chance to mount a defense. Afterward, the contestant has the choice of pressing an

"I forgive you" button or one that says "You're guilty!" While the contestant is deciding, suspenseful music is played as the audience divides into contesting groups, one side yelling "forgive 'em, forgive 'em" while the other shouts "nail 'em, nail 'em." This gives the show the quality of a soccer match in which rioting is about to erupt at any moment.

Place the Blame emerged as a leading game for Ron during a coaching session. When I met him at the door, he told me he'd had a breakthrough and was eager to share it.

Ron: "Yesterday, I realized that most of my unhappiness is my dad's fault."

Bob: "Ron, I want you to know that this is not the first time I've heard this kind of story. In fact, I'm writing a book called *Honest, It Wasn't Me: Three Thousand and Fifty-Two Compelling Ways to Blame Others for Your Misery*. I know you want to blame your dad and I'm sure he messed up your life a bit, but blaming him is going to work against you, not for you. Know why?"

Ron: "Not really."

Bob: "By blaming your dad for your unhappiness, you get to feel like a martyr. Being a martyr means you get to feel special for having to endure something someone did to you."

Bright, red spots began to appear on Ron's neck, and his face grew flushed and tense.

Ron: "You're a first-class asshole! No, I mean second class!"

Ron was pissed off, but his little revision broke us up. Laughing together helped to lighten the situation.

Bob: "Ron, one of my goals in life is to be a second-class asshole, because first class has never been my thing. I'm from the blue-collar world, you see."

Ron: "Okay. I'm sorry. Maybe you're third class."

Bob: "I'm happy to be a third-class asshole if you'll wake up and take responsibility for your unhappiness and quit feeling your whole life has been a grade B movie about martyrdom.

CHAPTER 4 — Placing Blame Is A Great Game

Your story reminds me of a headline I saw in one of the national tabloids. It said, 'Terribly unhappy person blames postman.'"

Ron (laughing): "That's absurd!"

Bob: "Yeah, but notice how you can't laugh at the story you've made up about your dad. I'm sure your dad made a few major contributions to your misery, but if you continue to believe that he screwed up your life, you're giving away your power to change it. As soon as you take responsibility for your unhappiness, you take that power back. Does this make sense?"

Ron: "How do I lose power by blaming him and get it back by taking responsibility?"

Bob: "By blaming your dad, you're saying the damage is done and there's nothing you can do about it. You'll remain a wounded person for the rest of your life by thinking there's no hope to change it. However, if you admit that you've chosen to be miserable, you take back the power to make new choices. In essence, you recover the hope and motivation to change yourself in positive ways. Is this sinking in?"

Ron: "I think it is. You're saying that by accepting responsibility for my unhappiness rather than blaming my dad, I'm creating the power to do something about it. That's amazing!"

Bob: "It is amazing, isn't it? Just think, by accepting responsibility, you quit being doomed to live an unhappy life. Instead, you recover the power to change yourself so you can create more happiness."

Ron: "What a liberating idea! Now I have hope that I can make some changes. Before, when I was sure it was my dad's fault, I felt helpless and hopeless. Now I know I can change. I can't tell you how free I'm feeling. I haven't felt this way for years!"

Bob: "Isn't that great? Now you'll be more optimistic, not pessimistic, about your chances to change. That's it for today. You've just taken a big step."

Ron: "This has been a life-changing experience for me. Thanks."

Bob: "Thank you. Remember that I'm just the coach, not the player. You're the guy on the field creating new moves."

Ron: "I'm sorry I called you an asshole. I was so angry I couldn't help it."

Bob: "Your anger was fine with me. In fact, anger can be a healthy release—as long as you keep your hands in your pockets."

Ron: "Does that mean I can call you an asshole anytime I feel pissed about something you say?"

Bob: "You can call me anything you want. It's just a bunch of words backed by a bunch of emotions."

The last time I saw Ron, I learned that he had gotten married. He told me he was creating a better way of thinking and living with his wife as his consciousness partner. I discovered that the turning point in his effort to change had been the day when he quit thinking his dad was the cause of his misery.

COACHING TIPS

- Instead of blaming others for your misery, accept responsibility for it yourself.
- Once you have accepted responsibility, notice how you're taking back the power to create new choices.
- From those choices, make changes in your thinking and your life so happiness increases. Be the power to make change.

CHAPTER 5

Beating Yourself Up With Stories

*"Fiction is fun to read,
but not always fun to live in."*
Barbara, corporate executive

Some unhappy people have a special torture chamber in their minds. Each day, they put themselves on the stretching rack by believing their negative thoughts and stories are true. Visiting mental torture chambers is perhaps only second to TV as a national obsession. In fact, it's a lot like TV because unhappy people become absorbed in the soap-opera lives they create for themselves. Becky was a drama queen when we first met. The name of her soap opera was *The Miserable Days of My Life*.

Becky was married to Brad, whom she'd fallen for in high school. One of her most glaring features was her tendency to dramatize her life. It took a lot of patience to be with her because she made herself miserable with her nightmare stories. In one of our early sessions, she laid out a tale about her life that had tragic highlights.

Becky: "When I think about the future, I'm sure nothing will work out. I keep thinking my marriage to Brad won't last, that I'll never find the job I really want, and that I'll live in misery the rest of my life. I'm a pessimist from top to bottom."

Bob: "Why do you tell yourself such dismal stories?"

Becky: "They're true."

Bob: "So you can predict the future?"

Becky: "I think I can see how things are going to turn out."

Bob: "You don't have the foggiest idea about your future. No one can predict the future. If they could, I'd take them to Las Vegas. You just make up stories and then convince yourself they're true. Why were you so certain about the stories you just told me?"

Becky: "Hmm, now that I think about it, it's obvious that I can't predict the future. No one can. So why did I make up those stories? I'm not sure."

Bob: "You make up stories because your mind loves certainty, even when it's unclear about the facts. So why do you make up stories about your future?"

Becky: "To fool myself into thinking that I know what's coming?"

Bob: "Brilliant! When you create positive stories, how do they make you feel?"

Becky: "They make me feel good."

Bob: "What about your negative stories?"

Becky: "Pessimistic and miserable."

Bob: "So what are you seeing about your stories?"

Becky: "I don't know for sure, but it's obvious that my stories have a big impact on me."

Bob: "When I was young, I was a fan of a TV series called

CHAPTER 5   Beating Yourself Up With Stories

'Dragnet.' It was a program with this guy named Sergeant Friday who took the lead in solving crimes. He understood a lot about the mind's desire for certainty and how human beings make up fiction, thinking they have the facts. When he questioned a witness, he would say 'Just the facts' several times. He did this because he knew that people make up fiction about everything, including what they think they saw."

Becky: "That reminds me of a story I told myself last week. A good friend promised that she'd come by to see me, but she didn't show up. I became really upset because I'd been looking forward to catching up with her. I created a big story about how she must have been upset about something I did. I ruined the rest of the evening worrying about it."

Bob: "Instead of worrying, what could you have done?"

Becky: "I was so convinced that my story was true, I'm not sure what else I could have done."

Bob: "Well, you could have stopped the storytelling and called her to get the facts."

Becky: "That didn't even dawn on me because I was so upset about it. Storytelling is so natural for me, how can I stop it?"

Bob: "When I'm unhappy, I use a practice I call 'The Three Boxes'. It's a way for me to think about my stories so I can stop telling them. It takes place in my imagination. When I open the first box, I see a note inside. It says, 'What is making you unhappy right now?' I think about the question carefully. When I have the problem nailed down, I open the second box. Inside, I find a note with another question, 'What's the story you've made up about your problem and how does it contribute to your unhappiness?' I look for the story and then I think about it as thoughts I've convinced myself are true. When I have my story down, I open the third box. Inside is another note that says, 'Stop telling the story and get the facts!'"

Becky: "You called 'The Three Boxes' a practice. What's

a practice?"

Bob: "A practice is a conscious effort we make to change our thinking, feelings, and behavior. The Three Boxes is a practice I created to help me stop my automatic storytelling so I can get the facts and a clearer view of reality."

Becky: "Let's see if I get this. A practice is like something new to do. You know, a new way to think, like 'The Three Boxes' will keep me from falling into my depressing stories. It will remind me to get all the facts."

Bob: "Yes, that's it. Quit the fiction writing! It's part of what's making you miserable, and who needs misery? It's like wearing shoes too small just to experience the pain."

Becky: "I guess I'd better get larger shoes because I'd like less misery."

Bob: "When you stop telling negative stories, something positive will happen. We pay a very big price for negative storytelling. The price is less happiness."

Becky: "I hope I'm smart enough to stop it."

Bob: "It will take awareness and effort, but you can do it."

A few weeks later, Becky told me about a practice she created. When she caught herself in a pessimistic story about her life, she would say, "Story time! Wake up and go get the facts!" This simple practice helped her stop whatever negative story she was telling. She also said her relationship with Brad had improved because she quit telling the story that their marriage wouldn't last. "When I started telling myself that I will make it last, in fact I will make it a lot better, I began to figure out ways to do that. As a result, Brad and I are getting closer."

CHAPTER 5 *Beating Yourself Up With Stories*

COACHING TIPS

- Notice when you've made up a negative story without knowing the facts and how you suffer from it.
- When you see what you're doing, stop the storytelling and get the facts.
- When you quit living in such negative stories about yourself, others, the future, and life, you'll become a happier person.
- If you can't help making up stories, then invent positive stories that make you feel good about yourself, others, your relationships, and your life.

Creative Sidetrack

It's time to take a sidetrack to crank up the creativity. My good friend, named Bill, has more creative currents flowing than anyone I know. We have a great time together. One day when I was talking about having to do yard work, he said, "What if, instead of saying 'I have to garden,' you said 'I get to garden?' What would happen?"

Bob: "What a great shift in thinking! If I always said 'I get to' instead of 'I have to,' I'd feel less trapped by my circumstances and more thankful for my opportunities."

Bill: "So what's your take on gardening now?"

Bob: "I feel lucky that my body and mind are in good enough shape to do gardening. It's not feeling like an obligation, but a privilege."

This encounter, which lasted no more than two minutes, changed my outlook. Now, when I start to think "I have to do" something, I say "I get to."

Think of at least two things you tell yourself you have to do. Shift your thinking to the idea that you get to do them.

What do you notice?

CHAPTER 6

Lower The Bar A Few Inches

"Perfectionism is the ability to quickly criticize your achievements to ensure that you never celebrate them."
Julie Ann, scientist

When fate deals the cards of life, some people get the perfectionist card and then have the special challenge of attaining a high level of success without going bonkers. It's actually not a bad card if you consider some of the others. How would you like to have been dealt the lazy card?

Perfectionists are cursed by having very high ideals. This means that everything—their behavior, their work, and their relationships—has to meet the highest standards. To achieve their lofty goals, they work much harder than most of the world's population. This ethic produces good quality work, recognition, status, and usually acclaim, if they can survive the pressures of always needing to shine and don't burn out from overwork.

Perfectionism produces unhappiness because it comes with harsh self-criticisms. Perfectionists live with an inner judge who keeps an eye on everything they do—how they speak, dress, look, write, live, and perform in a variety of situations. This judge is hell on wheels, possessing the uncanny ability to stay on the heels of perfectionists no matter how fast they run to get ahead.

Perfectionism is not just a personal thing. Look at our culture's emphasis on perfection, and you'll find it messing up many people's minds and lives. Think of the degree of perfectionism in the field of fashion alone, where models are tall and slender with faces made up to appear flawless. Watch a Miss Universe contest to see this punishing trend on a global scale as women parade around with their perfect bodies, perfect smiles, and perfect manners.

Men are also drawn into the perfectionism game, as a visit to any gym will show. Pumping iron to craft the perfect body takes countless hours, grunts, groans, a huge tolerance for boredom, and lots of time admiring the results in front of mirrors. Yet thousands of men across the country show up each day for these doses of torture.

Don't get me wrong. I have nothing against ideals because they help us determine whether we're succeeding or screwing up. When our lives come close to fulfilling our ideals, we know we're doing something right. When they don't, we know we're screwing up. By their nature, ideals are lofty, which means we'll always fall short no matter how hard we struggle to reach them. This makes screwing up inevitable. Screwing up makes unhappiness inevitable.

Anita was a perfectionist who had already achieved a lot in her life, first as a student with close to a 4.0 grade average and then as a career woman, but she was always down on herself.

CHAPTER 6

Lower The Bar A Few Inches

She came to see me because, given her achievements, she should have been happy but wasn't. With blonde hair, blue eyes, a broad smile, and perfect teeth, she looked like a fashion model.

From our first day together, it was clear that Anita was selling an image of the perfect woman. She dressed in the latest fashions and smiled often to convince me that she was happy. If you've been around a person who smiles constantly, you'll know what I mean when I say that Anita had become an expert at public relations. Although I knew she was putting on a show, I still liked her. Below the surface of her managed appearance, she had a spirit that sparkled. One day on an impulse, I decided to focus on her perfectionist ideals because I knew they were making her unhappy.

Bob: "Anita, since our first meeting, I've noticed how your ideals create a fair amount of misery for you. It might be good to talk about them."

Anita: "What's wrong with having ideals?"

Bob: "We can't help having them, but when they have us by the throat, it's a different matter. Most people fail to notice how much their ideals make them suffer. Perfectionists are especially vulnerable to this kind of torture. Would you say you're a perfectionist?"

Anita: "No doubt about it. I know I'm a perfectionist, but I don't like admitting how much I suffer from it. It would force me to change in some dramatic ways, and that really scares me."

Bob: "Isn't that why we're working together?"

Anita: "I guess so."

Bob: "We all have inner judges who are experts at finding our faults and then harping about them. How does your judge seem to you?"

Anita: "I'd say he's a brute of a guy, about fifteen feet tall and four feet wide. Perfectionists must be scared to death of their inner judges because they're afraid of being punished by them when they fail to do things in a perfect way."

Bob: "Is it fear of being punished, or is there something deeper going on?"

Anita: "I don't know."

Bob: "Close your eyes and look for an answer."

Anita: "I'm not convinced that will help, but I'll give it a shot."

Bob: "Take your time."

After about five minutes, Anita opened her eyes.

Anita: "While I was thinking about my perfectionism, I decided to talk to my judge to see if he knew what the deeper issue is for me. He said, 'First, you need to understand that I'm your creation. You invented me to ensure that you perform at the highest level. I force you to focus on your shortcomings all the time. As a result, you never feel good about yourself. This makes it hard for you to really like yourself. Not liking yourself enough, you have a hard time believing others when they say that they like you. How can they like someone who's not perfect? That's the question I put in your mind to torment you.'"

Bob: "Your judge laid it on the line. What are you seeing now?"

Anita: "I'm seeing that my perfectionist tendencies have a tragic undertone. Since I have a hard time liking myself because I'm so self-critical, I'm doomed to seek happiness and always fail. Is there a way out of this?"

Bob: "What way out do you see?"

Anita: "Understanding what I just said helps. Now I know how my perfectionist streak runs through my life and why it makes me miserable. If I laugh about it, maybe I can gradually lower the bar a few inches."

Bob: "You're coming to an important understanding, but you haven't mentioned how your perfectionism affects your relationships. What about that?"

Anita: "Hmm, that's a very tough question. I think my

perfectionism affects my relationships in two ways. Feeling that I'm flawed, I fear I'll be disliked and eventually rejected by others. Getting too close to someone increases my fear of rejection, so I keep myself at a safe distance. Since I apply my perfectionist standards to others, it's easy for me to find something to criticize about them. So my relationships start out well but often end up as disasters. This reminds me of a movie I saw recently. There was a scene where, in a moment of desperation, this perfectionist says, 'My perfect mate is the person I'll never meet.' That really hit me because I often feel that way."

Bob: "So as you lower the bar, your relationships should improve."

Anita: "I hope so."

Bob: "Perfectionism is strange because it works against one of the things perfectionists want, which is to be happy. Wanting the perfect body, the perfect personality, the perfect relationship, the perfect wedding, perfect children, and a perfect career will ensure a perfectly miserable life because humans will always fall short of perfection. Did you know that Persian carpets contain a defect so the weavers can avoid the arrogance of appearing to possess the perfection of the divine?"

Anita: "I've never heard that, but I like the idea. Seeing and living with my imperfections would be a good thing for me."

Bob: "What do you notice about your ideals and the idea of 'good enough'?"

Anita: "I'm not sure what you mean."

Bob: "Isn't it true that high ideals tend to make us believe that we're not good enough, others aren't good enough, and life isn't good enough? Living with the idea of 'not good enough' creates a fair amount of misery."

Anita: "I've definitely been living with the idea of not good enough. Seeing this, I don't know if I want to scream, cry, or laugh."

Bob: "What about all three at once?"

Anita: "Okay, Bob, now that you made me laugh, my problem does feel a bit less serious."

Bob: "I see light coming out of you."

Anita: "A few rays maybe."

Bob: "Enlightenment doesn't have to be a sudden shift of being. It can be a series of little enlightenments that produce changes that free us from living in automatic. I think you've just had a little enlightenment."

Anita: "It feels that way."

Bob: "A few years ago, I spent some time with a man in his seventies who had overcome years of anguish as a result of his perfectionism. One day, he said something that struck me as a little enlightenment. 'A bit of imperfection gives me the right to pass gas without beating myself up about it.' You know what I'm thinking, Anita? There should be a ten-step program for perfectionists because it has all the markings of an addiction. When people join, they'd get one of my T-shirts. The front would say, 'Hooked on perfection'. The back would read, 'You'll never hear me pass gas.' What do you think?"

Anita: "It embarrasses me to say this, but if I'd pass a little gas and get caught, I would make all the perfectionists feel a bit better about themselves."

Bob: "Remember, the idea that imperfection is bad was invented by perfectionists."

The next time we met, Anita handed me a large piece of newsprint. I couldn't help laughing when I opened it. It was a crayon drawing of her inner judge with several mouths, all shouting complaints about her. She had crossed out the judge and his criticisms. Underneath the drawing she had written, "It doesn't have to be perfect, just good enough."

CHAPTER 6
Lower The Bar A Few Inches

COACHING TIPS

- If your ideals are too lofty, lower them a bit. Doing so will give you more freedom, less stress, less guilt, and greater success, because you won't be beating yourself up all the time with self-criticisms.
- Keep working to prove your value, but not so hard that you make yourself miserable. Trying, but not too hard, will give you moments of relaxation so you can move into action again with a lot more energy and enthusiasm.
- Instead of thinking you and your work have to be perfect, use Anita's standard of "good enough." When you know that you're good enough, others are good enough, and life is good enough, your happiness will grow in a hurry.

CHAPTER 7

There Should Be A Law Against Put-Downs

"Who needs enemies when we have ourselves?"
Jon, bus driver

In football, it's illegal to make a chop block. That's when you hit a player behind the knees, which can cause career-ending injuries in a second. I wish there was a similar law against chop blocking others and ourselves with put-downs. If you're more miserable than you want to be, you're probably still run by your ideals, which will make you adept at the game of put-downs. To usher in a change, I propose a weekly holiday. It will fall on Fridays so people would be in a great mood for weekends. The holiday will be called "No Put-Downs Day."

Imagine how good we'd feel after a whole day's vacation from undercutting others and ourselves. Even the thought of it makes me feel good. Damn! I just heard from my realist. "Bob, will you please wake up and face reality? People must enjoy putting themselves and others down or why would they do it so often? It's like a game they play where the winner is the one left standing."

Put-downs are part of a much larger family of negative thoughts that make us feel wretched. For example, many people live in identity stories full of negative things they say about themselves. When people put too many of those negative judgments into their identities, they have to experience the consequences of what they created on a daily basis. It's a bit like a monster movie, and they become the monsters they created. This is what I told Roxanne when she laid out the various ways she put herself down. Although she criticized herself as part of her daily ritual, she was smart and had a good sense of humor.

Bob: "Roxanne, I've noticed since we started working together that you put yourself down a lot. I'm wondering if that's part of your identity story."

Roxanne: "I hate to think it is, but I also know there's an element of truth to it. I've created a story about myself with a fair number of negative sidelines that make me more wretched than I want to be. I have positives, but the negatives keep showing up to irritate and undermine me."

Bob: "So what's the story you tell about your identity?"

Roxanne: "On the positive side, it reveals what I like about myself. This includes my courage, my willingness to learn, my sense of humor, and my belief that I'm basically a kind person. On the negative side are thoughts that I'm not very interesting, not attractive enough, irritable, depressing to be around, and often too lazy. I feel so unworthy at times that I can't believe anyone could love me. I'm an anti-valentine."

Bob: "Do you know what gives this identity story the power to make you miserable?"

Roxanne: "Not really."

CHAPTER 7 — *There Should Be A Law Against Put-Downs*

Bob: "You think the negative thoughts in your story are true. By believing they're true, you give them power to make you unhappy."

I watched as Roxanne took a deep breath and then released a large reservoir of tension that had been building up in her. Tears began welling in her eyes.

Bob: "Take some time with this. It's important."

I handed her a box of tissues, and she took a handful.

Bob: "Would you like to take a break?"

Roxanne: "Yeah, that would be nice. I need to sort out my feelings and pull myself together."

I left the study and went to the kitchen to get a drink of water. After several minutes, I went back to the study with a glass of water for her. She thanked me and said she was ready to go on.

Bob: "What was coming up for you?"

Roxanne: "At first, I wanted to deny what you said about how the negative thoughts I put in my identity hurt me. Then I started to see your point. This made me feel terrible because I realized how I've wasted a good part of my life living in a negative story about myself with underlying themes of failure and disappointment. I've had happy times for sure, but way too many painful ones. What really gets to me is the fact that I made up the story that's making me miserable."

Bob: "Would I be right to say that you've become a good book of fiction with a bit of a horror twist?"

Roxanne: "That sounds pretty close."

Bob: "Would you like to hear a similar story?"

Roxanne: "Sure."

Bob: "A few years ago, I met a young woman I'll call Jen. She wasn't in coaching sessions with me but was someone I met by chance. In a conversation we had, she said, 'I'm not an interesting person and people don't like me, even those who say they're my friends.' I asked why she made up her identity that way. With a touch of anger, she said, 'What do you mean? It's the truth! I'm not interesting and people don't like me!' When I asked her to think about her story as a convincing piece of fiction, not the truth, she exploded. 'You're saying that I'm making all this up, that I'm creating my own suffering! I don't believe you! I'm pissed that you're pushing me to accept something I don't believe!'"

Roxanne: "She had a story that would make anyone unhappy."

Bob: "You know, Roxanne, if she had given a title to her identity story at that time, it would have been 'No living soul could like this woman.' However, I didn't give up on her because I sensed that she wanted to become more aware. About a half-hour later, with me coaching gently at crucial moments, she finally realized the part she had played in creating her nightmare story. Knowing she was ready for the next step, I asked her how she would change it."

Roxanne: "What did she say?"

Bob: "Instead of thinking she wasn't a person others could like, she decided to accept the idea that people would learn to like her when they got to know her better. A few months later, I learned that, as she shared more of herself with others, she began to attract people who appreciated who she was. Instead of trying to get people to like her, she became more sensitive to what she liked about herself. She told me, 'When I realized that I liked me, others began to like me. Now, I have good friends and I'm looking toward the future with confidence.'"

Roxanne: "That's an inspiring story. Now, I see what's possible for me."

Bob: "What is possible for you? How can you create a story about yourself that supports, rather than undermines you?"

Roxanne: "I guess I'm going to have to be a lot more

CHAPTER 7   *There Should Be A Law Against Put-Downs*

positive."

Bob: "Are you willing to work with me on this?"

Roxanne: "Sure."

Bob: "Okay. When you have a negative thought about yourself, what happens?"

Roxanne: "I start feeling terrible, and sometimes I get so depressed I withdraw from life."

Bob: "Have you ever thought about the fact that you're a human chain reaction?"

Roxanne: "I don't get it."

Bob: "Think of it this way. We become happy or sad based on the chain reaction of three things: thoughts, emotions, and behavior. For example, let's say you have a thought, 'I'm really a kind person at heart.' What will that thought produce?"

Roxanne: "It will make me feel good about myself."

Bob: "Right. The positive thought will produce a positive emotion. When you're feeling good about yourself, what kind of behavior will that create?"

Roxanne: "I'd probably be more social and treat myself and others better."

Bob: "So when you behave in a positive way, how does that affect the way you think?"

Roxanne: "If I treat myself better, I'm likely to think I must be a valuable person to treat myself that way."

Bob: "Okay. Here's the coaching. To become happier, create positive thoughts, positive emotions, and positive behaviors. Wherever you start in the chain, as long as it's positive, it will make you more positive, which is one of the main things that make people happy."

Roxanne: "It seems so easy when I think about what Jen did, but I have doubts that I'll be able to do it."

Bob: "It's because you aren't looking far enough into the future. Change happens over time if you take the first step and then keep moving forward. Start by watching what you say about yourself. When you catch yourself in a negative thought, remember the chain reaction and then move into positive thoughts, emotions, or behavior."

Roxanne: "I'll give it my best shot, but I know this won't be easy."

Bob: "If becoming happier was easy, you'd see everyone walking down the street with genuine smiles on their faces. Changes that produce happiness take hard work. There's no magic cure for anything. Are you willing to take up the challenge?"

Roxanne: "I'll do my best."

Bob: "Doing your best is all that life asks from you. It's also usually enough to make you happier. Just think about what you've learned already! Very impressive, I'd say."

Roxanne: "Thanks, Dr. Bob. I am very determined to change."

Bob: "You will, but it'll take time, so be patient."

A couple of years after we finished our work together, Roxanne created a stand-up comedy routine. It had a good run at a local theater and drew good-sized audiences. The name of the show was "And you think you're nothing." I went to one of her performances. She was great! During her routine, she drew the audience into some of the issues we worked on together. I especially liked her opening lines to the put-downs part of the show. "When other people wake up in the morning, they write down a list of things they'll do that day. I write down a list of reminders to fuel my put-downs. What do you think was at the top of my list today? 'Don't forget your fat thighs!'"

I loved how she made fun of herself and how she laughed about the things that make all of us miserable. I remember thinking at the time, "If people laughed at their put-downs like Roxanne, they'd turn up their happiness in a minute."

CHAPTER 7 — There Should Be A Law Against Put-Downs

COACHING TIPS

- Instead of putting yourself and others down, pull yourself and others up with positive thoughts. When a negative thought arises in your mind, throw it out like you would garbage and bring in a positive thought to replace it. Celebrate every day as a "No Put-Downs Day."
- Instead of making your identity story into a torture chamber full of negative qualities that undermine you, create a positive story that supports you.
- To stop your negative chain reactions, create positive thoughts, emotions, and behavior.
- Instead of taking yourself too seriously, be more like Roxanne and learn to laugh at yourself.

Creative Sidetrack

Thoughts are energy coming from the brain into awareness. How would you like to use that energy to make yourself happier? Instead of being taken over by your thoughts, take them over. Shape them.

Create three positive thoughts about yourself.

Create three positive thoughts about your social relationships.

Create three positive thoughts about life.

Create three positive thoughts about your potential to become happier.

What impact did those thoughts have on you?

CHAPTER 8

Self-pity Creates Some Great Whining

"I used to feel that life was picking on me, so I whined a lot. But, as I've gotten older, I changed. Now I'm sure it's picking on me."
Mona, jewelry designer

After I left the comedy circuit, I wallowed in self-pity for a while because I didn't know what to do with my life. One day when I was feeling especially sorry for myself, I saw some graffiti in a public restroom that made me realize I wasn't alone. On the wall, some guy had scrawled, "I'm where life dumps its sewage." Next to it, another guy had written, "I'm glad to see someone else using self-pity to get through the day." I told my counselor, Sophie, about the graffiti and how they made me want to do something about my plight. She said something like, "You know, Bob, self-pity is the mother of whining, and whining is the mother of misery. By complaining about how life is against you, you struggle against life, which is an open road to misery. Stop telling your 'poor me' story so you can reduce the whining. When you do, you'll become a happier man."

I always appreciated how Sophie didn't beat around the bush. I got her point right away, but it took quite a while to make the change. When I succeeded in setting aside self-pity as a crutch, I started to notice other people using it to get through their days. Sometimes I tried to help them get out of it, knowing that self-pity wasn't a good place to hang out.

Brady was one of the people I helped. I met him through a friend. After being with him for a short time, I saw a cloud of gloom hovering over his head. At first, I couldn't put my finger on his problem. Yet each time I saw him, I wondered why he was so negative. One day it hit me: He felt sorry for himself. Self-pity had him by the throat, and he didn't know it.

I asked him if he was willing to meet with me for a coaching session. I told him I might be able to elevate his happiness a bit. He hesitated until I said there wouldn't be a charge and we'd only meet once. I was pleasantly surprised when he agreed. He came to my place the following week. When Brady was comfortably seated, he said, "Well, what's up, Dr. Bob? You said you wanted to talk to me."

Bob: "How would you like to play a game of wake up?"

Brady: "What's that?"

Bob: "I get to say something honest to you, and then you get to wake yourself up. Want to play?"

Brady: "I guess so."

Bob: "When are you going to quit feeling sorry for yourself?"

A look of surprise passed across Brady's face. He started to deny what I said, but then he stopped to think. I could tell from his expression that he was seeing something.

Brady: "I'm having a hard time accepting this, but I also know you're right. I've been feeling sorry for myself for a long

CHAPTER 8 — Self-pity Creates Some Great Whining

time."

Bob: "What leads you to fall into self-pity and whine about how life is picking on you?"

Brady: "I'm not sure why, but I've always felt picked on, like the cards of life are stacked against me. My parents are fine, so I can't blame them. Maybe I was born with a tendency toward doom and gloom. Who knows? Then something happened recently that didn't help. A woman I'd been dating for a couple of months told me that she didn't want to see me anymore. When I asked why, she said that I wasn't fun to be around. That was a blow; let me tell you! Lately, it seems like life is pushing me around just to see how much punishment I can take."

Bob: "Out of all the people in the world, you've been chosen for special abuse. Is that it?"

Brady: "It feels that way sometimes."

Bob: "You enjoy feeling sorry for yourself and then whining about how life is stacked against you. This tendency is not going to make you many friends."

Brady: "I've had people tell me I'm a hard guy to be around. A friend even told me once that I was the only person she knew who could compete with her for the title of World's Champion Whiner. I'll bet you hear a lot of whining in your line of work."

Bob: "More than I'd like. I've even thought about inventing a machine I'd keep in my study called the 'Poor Me Meter.' It would be a sensitive device that would pick up every bit of whining a person did during a session. When the hour was up, the machine would give a rating, like, 'Off the charts whining today,' 'Superb whining,' 'Moments of great whining,' 'Not much whining,' 'Forgot to whine,' and 'Actually chose not to whine.' The rating would be printed on a nice-looking award that I'd give out at the end of a session. Would you like to know the best part of the Poor Me Meter?"

Brady: "Sure."

Bob: "I'd be paid according to the amount of whining a person did. Imagine how good it would feel to survive the most 'Poor Me' outbreak knowing that, with each sorrowful whine, I'd be filling my pockets with money. Instead of asking 'How have you been doing?' at the beginning of a session, I'd ask, 'Have any whining to do today?' Having to pay for each whine, imagine the changes that would occur in people! Hey, what about coming up with some of the things people whine about?"

In a few of minutes, we came up with a long list, like the following:

- Having to go to work
- Actually having to do some work
- Not having interesting work to do
- Not liking the boss, co-workers, and custodians
- Hating commercials on TV
- Having to listen to other whiners, who may whine even more than we do
- Having to pay taxes
- Worse yet, having to do taxes
- Having birthdays after forty

Brady: "'Poor Me' as a way of living is the ability to make up enough complaints to cultivate one acre of hell. I know because I've been living there."

Bob: "This reminds me of a conversation I overheard once. An elderly woman was having lunch with a friend, and they were talking about another woman who was a professional whiner. One of them said, 'If she ever gets into heaven, she won't like it there.' Of course she won't! Heaven will be hell for whiners because there wouldn't be anything to whine about. Let's face it. Whining is fun. If it wasn't, why would it be such a popular pastime?"

CHAPTER 8 — *Self-pity Creates Some Great Whining*

Brady: "I wonder where that leaves me."

Bob: "Where does it leave you?"

Brady: "When I'm unhappy, it feels like life is picking on me. Yet I know that 'Poor Me' is a story I can stop telling. When I do, I'm sure I'll appreciate more of what I have, which should make me happier. Being happier, I'll be less inclined to complain. Does this make sense?"

Bob: "It does to me. You'll also be a lot more fun to be around, so your relationships should improve."

Suddenly, the energy in the room changed. Brady and I looked at each other, wondering what was happening. There was a strange hissing sound and then a smell that seemed to be a mixture of humor, aftershave, and anxiety. To our surprise, Woody Allen stepped into the study, walked sheepishly across the room, and sat down beside Brady. Brady was stunned, and I was thinking, "Woody Allen visiting? I can't believe it!"

Woody said to Brady, "Look, kid, it's time to grow up, but don't think it's going to be easy. I've been at it for years. One thing I've learned is that if people were smart, they'd skip the teens and twenties. Those are the years when we're tested to see how we handle excessive self-pity. Some people never get beyond that point and feel sorry for themselves until the day they die. One of the things I love about death is that, if we don't get rid of self-pity while we're still kicking, death takes care of it when the kicking stops."

Brady: "I've never thought about death that way, but I see your point. It certainly fixes the problem of self-pity when we can't fix it ourselves."

Woody: "Sure does. Yet there's also a positive side to self-pity."

Brady: "What's that?"

Woody: "You get to knock yourself down while blaming life for it. It's quite a clever trick and definitely makes life interesting."

Having said his piece, Woody patted Brady on the shoulder and then got up to leave. Halfway across the room, he stopped, turned, and pointed at Brady, "Remember that self-pity can't exist at the same time as a smile."

Brady: "Thanks."

Looking as if he had just finished an Academy Award performance, Woody disappeared.

Bob: "What a surprise! I have other movie stars show up from time to time, but this is the first time Woody has visited. I was really impressed by what he said. He's a lot wiser than many people realize. He comes on funny but, when you look behind it, there's wisdom."

Brady: "Yeah. I guess I'd better follow his advice. I've been feeling sorry for myself too much and for too long. I'm going to put a stop to it."

Bob: "It'll make you more positive, so be prepared for the surprises that come when you experience more happiness. I hope you'll be ready for them. Most people don't know what to do with that much happiness."

Brady: "I'll be ready."

In less than an hour, Brady made an important turn in his life. A week later, he stopped by to thank me and give me a gift. Knowing I liked to add inscriptions to T-shirts, he had made one for me at a local shop. The front said, "Turn off your whining machine now!" The words on the back were, "Instead of thinking 'Poor Me,' think 'Lucky Me.'" He told me that, having quit playing the game of "Poor Me," others noticed right away that he was more upbeat and easier to be around.

CHAPTER 8   *Self-pity Creates Some Great Whining*

COACHING TIPS

- Stop feeling sorry for yourself because you think life is picking on you.
- Turn off your whining machine now!
- Instead of thinking "Poor Me," think "Lucky Me."

CHAPTER 9

Vampires And Angels

"Life is a cafeteria where humans enjoy feeding and getting fed. There are people who always want help and people who are ready to give it. It's a feeding partnership by which they help each other get through the day."
Laurie, school counselor

With effort, people experiencing too much misery will become happier in one week, although the prospect would probably worry them. They might feel anxious about how they will fill the time they've devoted to being unhappy and helpless. I'd say to them, "Don't worry, you'll find other things for your mind to do. You'll be able to start all kinds of new hobbies, like collecting old beer cans, making quilts, singing in a choir, or restoring old cars that should have gone to the junkyard. One of the things you might do is become more generous."

WHY AM I SO **DAMN** UNHAPPY?   *James Downton, Jr., Ph.D.*

Asking unhappy people to be generous has as much chance of succeeding as preserving ice cubes in hell. Know why? In their desperate need for help, unhappy people become so greedy for the generosity of others that they have a hard time giving back. Some may even drain the life force from their families and friends like vampires, taking time and energy from anyone who's willing to give it. I'm happy to say that generosity is about giving to others, not draining them dry.

Let's get to the heart of the issue with a question. What is generosity? It's what we do to care for others and ourselves. It's what people give to their unhappy friends by spending hours listening to them talk about their problems and the reasons they feel powerless to solve them. The people who help are angels, beings of light with big enough hearts to be generous.

Being an angel seems like a good deal, but it has a down side because it comes with a binding contract. The contract says in very small print, "Yours is a selfless mission. You are required to help others. To withhold help means the gates of heaven will be closed to you."

While being an angel makes caring people feel good, it can also be a source of misery because, given the binding contract, they feel guilty if they utter the forbidden word "No" to requests for their help. However, if they overdo helping, they can reach a point where they resent the people they feel obligated to serve. Of course, they'll have a hard time admitting that to themselves because resenting the people they help will be at odds with their angelic self-images. Angels have to look really good and feel even better.

Having seen the problems angels face, let's turn to the vampires. One of the interesting things about vampire people is that they either don't know that's what they are or, if they do, they won't admit it. It's a vampire survival mechanism. The unhappy people who drain their friends dry are vampires. They'll take as much time, energy, and money from others as

CHAPTER 9

Vampires And Angels

they can get.

A case in point was Tandy. When we first met, she was dressed in a new-age style with crafted jewelry and hand-tied fabrics. Given her appearance, I was surprised to discover how unhappy she was. She laid out her problems, hoping to convince me how horrible they were and how much she suffered from them. No matter what issue we covered, she felt helpless to change herself or her circumstances. During our third meeting, when she was trying to get my sympathy about another tragedy in life, I laid it on the line.

Bob: "Are you a vampire?"
Tandy: "Are you crazy?"
Bob: "Just enough to be free. Well, are you a vampire?"
Tandy: "No, I'm not a vampire. Do I look like one?"
Bob: "You might be a vampire and not know it, so now is the time to take the vampire test!" I walked over to my desk, took out a test, and handed it to her with a pencil. "Fill this out as honestly as you can and then we'll talk."

VAMPIRE TEST

Do you express how unhappy you are to anyone who will listen?

Yes [ ] No [ ] Well, maybe [ ]

Do you complain a lot to others?

Yes [ ] No [ ] Well, maybe [ ]

Do you make others know how helpless you are to solve your problems?

Yes [ ] No [ ] Well, maybe [ ]

Do you believe that life is picking on you and tell everyone as

WHY AM I SO **DAMN** UNHAPPY? James Downton, Jr., Ph.D.

often as you can?

Yes [ ] No [ ] Well, maybe [ ]

Do you ask people for help and special favors a lot more often than you give them?

Yes [ ] No [ ] Well, maybe [ ]

Add up your scores, giving a five to any "Yes" and a three to any "Well, maybe."

If you have a score of thirteen or more, welcome to the Vampire Club! A new Web site is being designed to serve you, where you'll be able to read horror stories people tell about themselves and their dreary, unfulfilled lives. You'll also be able to purchase a sharp set of plastic vampire teeth and sinister capes for all occasions.

Bob: "So what was your score?"

Tandy: "I'm not a vampire."

Bob: "I'll bet you got a high score and don't want to admit it."

Tandy: "No matter what this test says, I know I'm not a vampire!"

I paused, looking for a good way to respond. I knew she was at a turning point, and I didn't want to screw it up. While I was wondering what to say, colorful sparks began flying around the room, randomly zapping the walls, furniture, and floor.

Bob: "It must be a visitor coming. I wonder who?"

Just as Tandy was about to say something, movie great Katherine Hepburn walked quickly into the room. Katherine was wearing a red dress to accentuate the fact that she was a powerful woman who said what was on her mind.

Katherine: "So Tandy, you deny being a vampire because you can't face the truth. Of course you're a vampire! You've taken more than your share of people's sympathy and support, that's for sure!"

CHAPTER 9 *Vampires And Angels*

Tandy: "No, I haven't!"

Katherine: "Will you please wake up and face the truth so you can change?"

Tandy looked down at her hands, fidgeting from nervous tension. She was struggling to decide whether she was going to continue to deceive herself or come out with the truth.

Katherine: "Come on, do yourself a favor. Admit that you've been a vampire for years."

Tandy: "Okay, okay. I guess I'll have to admit to a few vampire tendencies, or you won't get off my back."

Katherine: "That's better. Now that you've faced the facts, what change will you make?"

Tandy: "I really don't know. Maybe I'll try to be more generous."

Katherine: "Do you mean it, or is this your way of feeling good about yourself for one minute and then forgetting you ever said it?"

Tandy: "I think I mean it."

Katherine: "Don't tell me that you think you mean it! That's a good sign you won't do it! Give me a real commitment! Come on, say you'll be more generous or give up one thing that gives you great pleasure, like watching TV or eating ice cream. If you can't make commitments to change, give up now because, without a real commitment, you'll stay the same. Do you see my point?"

Tandy: "Okay. I'll become more generous. Does that satisfy you?"

Katherine: "No! You have to say what you'll give up if you fail to stay committed."

Tandy: "If I fail, I'll give up the thing I adore, not half-heartedly, but with devotion. I'll give up drinking coffee."

Katherine: "That'll do it."

As Katherine left the room, she patted Tandy on the shoulder to finalize the deal and reassure her.

Bob: "What's your take on that?"

Tandy: "What a great force of nature! Katherine was unrelenting. Make a real commitment or give up! After all these years of thinking I was doing something about my unhappiness, I'm realizing now that I've never been deeply committed to making a change. My commitments have been 'maybes,' not 'definitely wills.' I learned from her that I have to develop stronger commitments to change; otherwise it's all big ideas with no results. I have to make and keep some promises, like being less of a vampire and being more generous."

Bob: "How will you be more generous?"

Tandy: "Instead of draining other people dry, I'll offer to help them. That will get me started."

Bob: "You know, Tandy, when we consider the nature of generosity, we think about leaving bigger tips and giving more to charities, yet money is just one of our currencies. Besides money, what other currencies do you have?"

Tandy: "I'm not sure what you mean by 'currencies.'"

Bob: "Think of them as personal resources, including money, which you have at your disposal to give away right now. Many of your currencies renew themselves so you have an infinite supply of them."

Tandy: "I'm still not following you."

Bob: "Should I tell you about the currencies I use? They're part of a practice I call 'the four chambers of a generous heart.'"

Tandy: "Yeah, that would help."

Bob: "Do you agree that being kind to yourself and others is one of your personal currencies?"

Tandy: "I have that ability, when I decide to use it."

Bob: "This is the first chamber of a generous heart. Imagine how much happiness you will create by treating yourself and others with kindness."

Tandy: "What's the second chamber?"

Bob: "'Appreciation.' I know you can show more appreciation for yourself and others. When you do, you'll see happiness grow within and around you. Relying on those two heart chambers alone will change how you feel about yourself and your life. The remaining two chambers, 'respect' and 'acceptance,' just make things better. Those four renewable currencies work together to expand generosity. Be kind to yourself and others, show appreciation and respect, and create an attitude of acceptance."

Tandy: "I like how this covers how we treat ourselves, not just how we treat others. If we appreciate others and not ourselves, we've missed the point."

Bob: "Absolutely! Many people find it easier to be generous toward others than toward themselves. That reminds me of a story. At a family gathering, a woman in her late twenties asked her grandmother if there was any hope for the world. What her grandmother said touched her.

'I'm a firm believer in the idea that the world changes when we change. I don't mean that all of the world's problems are solved magically. I mean that if we've been living in misery, we have the power to make positive changes. Those changes create waves of goodness that will eventually cover the world.'"

Tandy: "That's a good story for me. I came today as a vampire, and I'm going to leave as a small wave of change."

Bob: "You bet. As you change, you'll alter the future of the world."

Soon after this session, Tandy told me that she had volunteered at a program through which food and other services are provided to families that have fallen on hard times. Her community service was having a positive impact on her. The problems she had, which seemed so big when we first met, became quite small in comparison to the problems of the people she served. She also enjoyed helping people who had serious survival needs, which gave her life meaning and made her feel better about herself. She became more angelic, and it made her a happier person.

COACHING TIPS

- Take the vampire test to find out whether you're one. If you are, quit draining people dry and be generous instead. If you're an angel, learn to say "No" so you won't end up resenting those you feel obligated to serve.
- To become more generous toward yourself and others, practice "the four chambers of a generous heart." Toward yourself and others, express kindness, appreciation, respect, and acceptance.
- Develop a commitment to change that will satisfy the lady in the red dress. Convert your "maybes" into "definitely wills."
- Follow Tandy's inspiration and volunteer in your community to help people with bigger problems than yours. It will give you a new perspective on your life as well as practice at being an angel. Both will make you happier.

Creative Sidetrack

Whew! We've just taken a walk through the land of self-pity and vampires. Sorry to be encouraging you to face these issues, but what is ignored can't be changed. You may be feeling a bit of despair at the moment, so what about creating some hope? It will help revive you for the important issues that lie ahead.

Hope does three things. It creates a feeling that things will get better, a vision of what life will be like when they do, and the motivation to turn the vision into reality. Take a minute to think about an issue that's making you unhappy and then answer the following questions to create hope.

When you start putting out effort to change, how are things going to get better for you?

What will your life be like when they do?

How will you stay in action to create what you want and need?

Someone once said: "A person without hope is a person without light." Now that you've turned up your light, you can look forward to change!

CHAPTER 10

Fears Are Knots Tying Up Your Mind

*"Fear is like getting a bad haircut.
You wish you didn't have it, but you do."*
Ramona, stockbroker

We hate to admit it, but fear dominates a good part of our lives. Isn't it fun to face reality as if by looking at a run-away truck, we could stop it from smashing us flat? As the truck approaches, I see a sticker on the front bumper. It says, "What you don't want to see is Re-al-ity." This message has a nice ring to it. Let's make it the opening lines of a song.

"What you don't want to see is Re-al-ity.
You know it hurts to have to face the facts.
You don't want to suffer but you want to relax.
So wake up now to escape your bind.
Your fears are knots tying up your mind."

How do your fears create knots in your mind? How will you untie them? We all know that our fear of death makes us pessimistic because the outcome of life is certain. No one survives it. Wanting to shore up your optimism, I have to tell you about a prophecy that was inscribed on an ancient tomb in Egypt. It said, "Death will be easier than sitting through a one-star movie." The fact is that there are a lot of things worse than death, like living forever or having to go out when you've just gotten the worst haircut of your life.

Everyone I coach ends up talking about their fears and how they influence what they think and do. Dana was a special case because she came to me to deal with her fears.

Dana: "Dr. Bob, I'm a professional worrier. I believe there's a disaster waiting to happen around every corner. This makes me tense and stressed out. I want to know more about my fears and how to deal with them so I can be happier."

Bob: "I'm impressed. Most people want to remain in the dark about their fears. So how do your fears affect your ability to be happy?"

Dana: "You can't be happy when you're afraid!"

Bob: "That's a great insight! You're seeing that fears are major contributors to your unhappiness. What are some of the fears that get to you?"

Dana (after pausing for a minute to think): "I'm afraid of walking along steep drop-offs on a hike, flying in airplanes in bad weather, failing to impress people, never finding a man I can really love, saying the wrong thing, saying the honest thing and regretting it, and I'm constantly afraid of being rejected or ridiculed by anyone."

Bob: "That's a good list and only a sample of the fears that drive us all nuts. Speaking of fear, I visited New York City a while ago. I learned in a hurry to be afraid of crossing the streets of Manhattan. Drivers there seem to enjoy putting you face-to-face with the granddaddy of all fears."

CHAPTER 10 *Fears Are Knots Tying Up Your Mind*

Dana: "What's that?"

Bob: "Death. I came close to having that experience a few times and felt good at the end for frustrating all those New York City drivers."

Dana: "It's interesting that I didn't have fear of dying on my list, but it's behind some of my other fears."

Bob: "Yeah, fear of death loves to sneak around. When you're experiencing a fear, what's going through your mind?"

Dana: "I'm sure that I'm going to make a mistake, fail, get hurt, or die."

Bob: "It didn't take you long to figure that out, because fear is always warning us about dangers. It yells, 'Look out! You're about to mess up or die!' Fear is like a guardian angel in our heads that's waking us up to the presence of danger. When our awareness of danger is at its peak, we're on full alert. We're looking right and left while our adrenalin is charging up so we're able to duck or take off at 6,000 miles per hour."

Dana: "What you just said makes me realize how much my fears control me. Like I said, I'm a professional worrier."

Bob: "If I told you to stop worrying, would you?"

Dana: "Not really because, by mentioning it, you'd be reminding me to worry. I'd probably start wondering what I needed to worry about."

Bob: "That's a great point! To tell people not to worry is about as effective as telling a woman who's concerned about her age that she looks beautiful. When you say, 'You look beautiful,' she starts thinking, 'But what about all those wrinkles around my eyes?' The same is true about telling someone not to worry. They hear 'Don't worry' and begin thinking, 'Yeah, but what about all the dangers?'"

Dana: "Is there any way out of this?"

Bob: "I'm glad you asked, because there is an exit. First, we have to understand the nature of fear as a thought. It automatically increases the probability of disaster in our minds.

The reason fears scare us so much is that they are usually exaggerations."

Dana: "I've never thought of my fears that way, but it's obvious that many are exaggerations."

Bob: "Let's have you do some work with that discovery. Starting with your earliest memory, how many of your fears came true? Close your eyes and think about it for a few minutes."

In about five minutes, Dana was back with me.

Bob: "What did you discover?"

Dana: "While reviewing my life, I found that what I feared rarely came true—maybe five percent of the time. While I was realizing how most of my fears were exaggerations, I had a strange experience. Knowing the picture of Humphrey Bogart was behind me, I imagined him standing halfway in the shadows of my mind. He stepped into the light and spoke to me. 'Hey, don't you get it? If your fears are exaggerations, then shrink 'em down so you can slap 'em around.'"

Bob: "Bogart was always smart in a streetwise way."

Dana: "Yeah, I can see his point, but there's something that bothers me. I can imagine shrinking down the size of my exaggerated fears, but what about the more realistic ones? The fact is that there are real dangers. How do I deal with them?"

Bob: "Good question. When you think you're facing a more realistic threat, it's still a good idea to consider how you might be exaggerating its potential to hurt you or those you love. If reducing the size of your fear doesn't do the trick, you have three other options. You can imagine the worst possibilities if the fear is justified, and then decide whether you can accept them. If you can, it will help you face your fear and take action. You can draw on your personal resources, like courage, to move ahead even though you're afraid. If those strategies fail, you can be smart and simply retreat from the danger."

Dana: "I think fear is one of the biggest obstacles

CHAPTER 10 — Fears Are Knots Tying Up Your Mind

between me and happiness. I'm scared of so many things that I get consumed by my worries. Getting beyond worry seems impossible."

Bob: "Our fears never go away completely because circumstances offer challenges to our security all the time. Some fears might be related to our physical survival, while others arise from our desire to look good, gain acceptance, and maintain control. Some of those are exaggerated fears that we can shrink down."

Dana: "I like the idea of shrinking down my exaggerated fears, but aren't there fears I should pay closer attention to because they're urging me to respond to danger?"

Bob: "Sure, some fears we need to deal with, like when we're in a car with someone who's driving too fast. We need to speak up!"

Dana: "So you're saying that I need to be smarter about my fears. If there are real dangers, I should take steps to deal with them. If my fears are exaggerations, I should shrink them down in size. Am I getting this right?"

Bob: "You've got it. The optimist in me would say, 'Managing our fears won't be a perfect solution, but even modest changes can improve our lives in a dramatic way.'"

Dana: "That's a good point. One thing that makes me unhappy is thinking that life should be perfect."

Bob: "Dana, the fact is that life is sloppy."

Dana: "Life is sloppy! I love that! It makes room for our fears and all the other things we wish didn't exist, but do."

Bob: "Since I know that life is sloppy, I'm going to buy myself some rubber boots."

Dana: "Get me a pair, will you?"

This was a crucial session for Dana. In one hour, she learned to evaluate her fears. Later, she told me about a practice she created to manage those fears. When she caught herself in a fear she knew was an exaggeration, she'd say, "Dana, shrink this one down so you can slap it around." She told me that this simple practice was improving her life.

COACHING TIPS

- Instead of automatically responding to your fears with worry, evaluate them. Which of your fears are pointing out real dangers you need to actively deal with or avoid? Which are exaggerations you can shrink down in size?
- Start with your earliest memory and go through your life to determine what percentage of the time your fears were realized. This will help you discover how many of your fears were exaggerated. Then think about how many of your current fears are blown out of proportion.
- To manage your fears so they don't automatically control you, reduce the size of the fear by considering the probability of it being realistic. If that doesn't work, think about the worst thing that can happen if your fear is realistic, and then ask whether you can accept it. If you can, you'll be freer to take action. If you can't, draw on your personal resources, such as courage, to act in the face of your fear. If all your strategies fail, know that you can retreat from the perceived danger.
- Think about the challenges you were afraid to take on and the opportunities you let slip by because of your exaggerated fears. Consider what you're willing to do now, given what you know about the exaggerated nature of fear as a thought.

CHAPTER 11

Going On Guilt Trips

> *"The only thing that can beat guilt for having a good time is not having it."*
> *Roberto, therapist*

Guilt comes with biting self-criticisms and the belief that we deserve to be punished. A Woody Allen character might say: "Guilt is the second-best way I punish myself. The first is trying to get a date." I know someone who feels guilty when she takes a bite of carrot cake with cream cheese frosting. Imagine the power that one little piece of carrot cake has over her. In our culture, fat has even greater power. Fat speaking: "Just adding two more pounds of me can make you feel guilty and miserable for two months. I'm the boss, let's face it."

Internally, guilt keeps us in line with our values, so we're able to feel good about ourselves at the end of the day.

Externally, guilt is a source of social control. It keeps us in line with social norms so we avoid getting into trouble with our peers, parents, religious authorities, and the police. This reminds me of a bumper sticker I saw recently. It said, "If you're not feeling guilty, you're not living right." You get the point of guilt when you reverse the two ideas, "If you're not living right, you should be feeling guilty."

Most of our guilt arises from our early relationships with religious figures, parents, grandparents, teachers, and, at times, older sisters and brothers. Those people were able to influence our deepest values because we admired, trusted, or feared them, which meant we allowed them to arrange our guilt trips. They were heaven's travel agents, because the guilt trips they booked for us reduced our chances of doing unpaid work for the Prince of Darkness. Some of the guilt trips serve us; others undermine us.

Guilt is a warning to straighten up and live right. In that way, it helps us avoid or stop screw-ups. People who are intolerant, abusive, and violent do mean things because they don't have that healthy kind of guilt or, if they do, they fail to respond to it. It's important for creating a decent life to let guilt show us where our ethical lines need to be drawn. Guilt of this healthy type keeps us in line with social morality so our lives work, we don't end up in jail, and we get periodic raises. In this way, guilt is good because it keeps us from being so stupid that we get into trouble or hurt people. My grandma used to say: "If you live clean, you won't have to die dirty." That wisdom has stuck with me.

Having seen the positive side of guilt, it's time to look at the other side. Getting to know lots of people as a happiness coach, I've learned there's also an unhealthy kind of guilt. It's the kind we develop about little things, like putting off writing a thank-you note. Guilty anguish about such misdemeanors can torment us, so working to overcome our guilt about little things

CHAPTER 11 — Going On Guilt Trips

is a good idea. But how do we do that?

Suzanne was a former Catholic who wanted to shake off the guilt left over from her religious training in childhood. The day we started talking about guilt, she said, "What the priests and nuns did to me may take the rest of my life to undo. They go to your core and plant seeds of guilt that start sprouting anytime you think about violating one of their tenets."

Bob: "You don't have to be a Catholic to have big guilt trips. Guilt seems to come to everyone through their ideals and morals."

Suzanne: "Well, I know I suffer a lot from guilt, and sometimes I'm sure I'll go to hell for being an ordinary person fulfilling my needs."

Bob: "If the devil suddenly showed up here, what do you think he'd say to you?"

Suzanne (laughing): "I'm reserving a place for you?"

Bob (also laughing): "You could ask him if he's saving you a house or an apartment."

Suzanne: "I'll bet it's a very small room without a view."

Bob: "If the devil spoke to you, what would he say?"

Suzanne (in a booming voice): "Suzanne, I have come to encourage you to be a professional, everyday sinner! Act with passion to satisfy every desire, no matter how destructive and depraved it might be! Unrestrained appetite without guilt, imagine your satisfaction! Don't listen to those who tell you to feel guilty when you're just following the impulses of your real nature!"

Bob: "Would you be convinced?"

Suzanne: "Not me. If I did what the devil said, priests and nuns would be at my house tomorrow. I'm impressed with the power of the devil's sales pitch, but seeing how sin can get me into hot water, I'd better stay on my guilt trips."

Bob: "The devil has a tough job. Since it's difficult for him to recruit people like you who believe they'll pay a big price for sinning, he has to go after people who don't believe in hell and who also have a strong inclination to break the rules. They're the ones who enjoy committing crimes, killing each other for no reason, and partying so hard until 4:00 a.m. that we can't sleep."

Suzanne: "Bob, if I were the devil, I'd say, 'Yes, I've got a hard job, but I like it. The hours are good, I get free room and board, and I'm constantly challenged to find creative ways to entice people to sin. Given all the hatred, violence, and wars in the world, I'd say that I'm doing a hell of a job. Probably about an A-minus on a four-point grading scale. Of course, I do have to acknowledge that, without men, I'd probably be performing at the D level.'"

Bob: "Suzanne, that was great! You should go into acting. And you were right about us guys. We make the devil's work a lot easier."

Suzanne: "This has been fun and revealing. Now I know that I'll avoid becoming a major sinner because I'm not going to take chances that might earn me admission into hell. Yet, there are things I do that make me feel guilty and miserable that are probably so small I shouldn't worry about them."

Bob: "What things?"

Suzanne: "All my ideals come with guilt trips. I feel guilty when I fail to keep my word to someone, postpone writing to family or friends too long, or make a complete fool of myself at a party. When I send a birthday card late, I feel guilty about that, too. Can you imagine a line of people waiting to get into hell for sending birthday cards late? That would be a very long line."

Bob: "Let's make a list of other things that make people feel guilty but wouldn't qualify them for admission into hell!"

After about ten minutes, we had a long list, including

- Hurting someone's feelings
- Telling a lie

CHAPTER 11 — Going On Guilt Trips

- Procrastinating
- Forgetting someone's birthday or anniversary
- Failing to respond to a friend's request for help
- Wasting too much time watching TV
- Eating too much
- Getting angry
- Being lazy

Suzanne: "Most of the things that make me feel guilty wouldn't qualify me for a place in hell. They're not nearly as deadly as the priests and nuns led me to believe. Just saying that isn't enough though. Is there something I can do to reduce my guilt?"

Bob: "Glad you asked. One way to reduce your guilt is to challenge the authority figures who planned your guilt trips over the little things. To achieve this breakthrough, use the 'tutu maneuver.' As you probably know, a tutu is a ruffled ballet skirt."

Suzanne: "I know what a tutu is, but what's a 'tutu maneuver?'"

Bob: "You close your eyes and imagine your guilt-inducing authority figure dancing around in a tutu. When you see how silly that person looks, you'll experience a sharp decline in your admiration, trust, and fear. This will reduce your guilt and increase your happiness."

Suzanne: "That sounds like a good strategy, but what if it doesn't work?"

Bob: "If you still feel twinges of guilt, practice the 'forgiveness and penance maneuver.' Sit in a chair with your hands on your knees and make fists. Open your left hand and, as you do, forgive yourself for what you did that's making you feel guilty. If you're still feeling guilty, open your right hand. As you do, create a penance with just enough punishment so your guilt debt is paid. Your punishment might be doing ten pushups or eating only three desserts that day. After establishing your plan for penance, close your eyes, focus on your breath, and give a simple word of thanks for being alive. If you can reduce your guilt about little things by ten percent this coming week, you'll see your happiness increase by thirty percent."

Suzanne: "How does that work?"

Bob: "Don't ask me. I just made it up. Yet, it seems reasonable to think that a small change can produce a big result. Well, that's it for today."

Suzanne: "This has been an intense experience. I'll let you know how much I can reduce my guilt in the next few days."

A few days later, Suzanne sent me a thank-you card with a funny poem she had written.

"Not Guilty!"
I imagined priests wearing pink tutus.
Several nuns showed up in tutus as well.
Seeing how silly they looked while dancing,
I laughed at their claims that I'd end up in hell.

COACHING TIPS

- If you're feeling guilty about serious ethical offenses, like hurting yourself or others, stop doing it! Your guilt is waking you up so that you can live a better life. Remember my grandma's wisdom: "If you live clean, you won't have to die dirty."
- If you live with too much guilt over little things, use the tutu and the forgiveness and penance maneuvers to reduce it.
- Reduce your guilt about the little things by ten percent in the next week so you can elevate your happiness by thirty percent.

Creative Sidetrack

Guilt and eating seem to hang out together. I know because sometimes I feel guilty for devouring too many chocolate malts in a month. I love them with a passion. When you love something that much, it becomes like a romance that you can't quit thinking about. In a weak moment, it can get the best of you.

Like the day I was cleaning the rain gutters on my house when the thought, "I'd love to have a chocolate malt" popped into my mind. The more I thought about it, the more my desire turned into malt lust. In less than an hour, I was at an ice cream shop consuming one of the really huge malts, the kind that comes in a metal container about the size of a bucket. If I always went for chocolate malts when the urge came over me, I'd need a sofa, instead of a chair, to sit on. Fortunately, I've found a creative way to shift my thinking to keep my romance with chocolate malts in check.

In the past, when I got an urge for a chocolate malt, I was completely focused on the first taste. I knew it was going to be delicious. Now when I have that thought, I shift my thinking to the last taste. What will follow the last taste? Probably a bit of guilt, the thought "I really didn't need that," and maybe slight nausea from the huge sugar and milk-fat injection. As soon as I shift to the last taste, my desire for the malt subsides just enough for me to make a freer choice about it. I've passed up dozens of malts this way, and that's why I can still sit in a normal-sized chair.

Don't get me wrong, I still have chocolate malts, but not every time I tell myself I want one. I've also used this practice with great effect to pass up bags of potato chips, doughnuts, and pie a la mode.

People have all kinds of food romances, which is why so many are getting too fat. Airlines may have to use more powerful engines so airplanes not only get off the ground but also stay there.

What unhealthy foods do you have a romance with?

What would happen if, rather than thinking about the first taste, you thought about the last one?

Take a moment to consider how you might use this practice in your eating life to reduce your guilt while you become a healthier and happier person.

CHAPTER 12

Up To Your Eyeballs In Lies

"Lying is an attempt to cover your ass with words."
Joe, bartender

People who live up to their eyeballs in lies pay a big price for it. Did you know there's a suburb in hell for liars? Only liars can live there, and the only rule they have to follow is never to tell the truth. Never telling the truth means they can't trust anyone and no one can trust them. Without trust, creating close relationships and a sense of community are impossible. Imagine living that way. Yet, there are people who destroy trust and emotional communion with others by lying. John's story is a good example of how lying may seem like a good idea under the pressure of circumstances, and how we eventually pay a price for it.

The day John came for his first session, I learned that he

was a successful businessman. He was married to Becky and had a nine-year-old son named Kyle. He was a big man, and he had an air of dominance combined with aloofness. He was struggling with stress and needed to find new ways to handle his over-committed life. He didn't know that lying was an issue for him until our fourth session.

He was twenty minutes late that day. When I answered the door, I said, "You're late. What happened?"

John: "I'm sorry. I got an urgent call from my mom just before I left the house."

I noticed that John avoided looking at me, which made me wonder whether he was telling the truth. I had to find out.

Bob: "I think you just lied to me. I don't believe you got a call from your mother."

As we made our way into the study, John looked nervous. I wondered whether he was inventing a way to respond to my challenge. As we were sitting down, he made a feeble attempt.

John: "My mom did call. Should I tell you what she said?"

Bob: "Look, I may be wrong, but I think you're lying. I believe that you were late for another reason. Maybe it was a good reason, but I doubt it given how hard you're trying to cover your ass. I'll bet you a five spot that you're lying and defending your lie automatically. Will you take the bet?"

John: "You're tough! Okay, I'll admit I was lying. I didn't get a call. I was late because I didn't pay enough attention to the time."

Bob: "Thanks. Having told the truth, you've moved into integrity with me. Now honesty rather than deceit is operating between us. If we tell the truth to each other, we'll trust each other. Trust is the golden thread that makes relationships work. I don't mean to lecture you, but there will be times when I have to lay out the truth for you to hear, whether you like it or not."

CHAPTER 12 Up To Your Eyeballs In Lies

John: "That's okay. Most people would have let me get away with lying. In the future, I'll try to tell the truth. You notice I said 'try' because sometimes I lie without thinking."

Bob: "Hey, there are times when we might choose to lie to make someone feel good or to protect ourselves and the ones we love. But lying to cover our ass? That kind we can give up."

John: "I'll think about that."

Bob: "Now you know that you lie without pausing to think."

John: "I lied to you because I didn't want you to think I was irresponsible."

Bob: "Right. Sometimes we lie to gain acceptance or avoid rejection. Since you started out lying, let's see how much you can reduce it during this session. Let's start with a simple idea. People know you lie, but they don't call you on it. Either they're afraid to confront you or they've accepted the social agreement that people don't call each other on their lies. I want you to know that I'm not one of those people."

John: "A real hard ass, huh?"

Bob: "Actually, the opposite. My ass is much softer than I'd like. But, as a happiness coach, I tell the truth so you can create a better way to live. Since I know that lying won't make you happy over the long haul, I'll call you on it."

John: "I need to have someone in my face, confronting me with my issues."

Bob: "Good. Let's get to work. How do you lie and why do you do it?"

John: "I'm feeling awkward about this."

Bob: "Of course, but we're working together for a good reason. I have to assume it's because you think I can help you create a happier life. So let's get back to my questions. How do you lie and why do you do it?"

John: "This is tough. I'm seeing what I've been hiding, even from myself."

Bob: "I know. Just give it your best shot. I appreciate you for wanting to do this. Most people can't face the truth. You're facing it."

John: "Okay. I need to push myself if I'm going to get anything out of this. In an argument with Becky the other day, I made up a few facts to convince her that I was right about an issue. What I said was pure bullshit, but I lied with such conviction that I don't think she noticed. I also lied to my son, Kyle, recently. I told him I'd attend an event at his school and then forgot about it because I was wrapped up in my work at the office. Instead of telling him the truth, I made up a story about how a crisis developed that I needed to take care of."

Bob: "You could have told him the truth. Why did you lie instead?"

John: "I didn't want him to know that I had forgotten something that was important to him. He might have thought that I didn't love him, and I love him a lot. I lied to Becky because I didn't want to lose the argument. I guess that's a control thing."

Bob: "How are your relationships with Becky and Kyle? Are they good, pretty good, or at the margin?"

John: "They're good."

Bob: "I doubt it. You think you're getting away with lying, but you aren't. They know that you lie."

John: "Damn! I just realized what I did last Saturday. I lied and then forced Kyle to lie for me. The phone rang and he answered it. It was a guy from the office calling for me. I didn't want to talk to him, so I told Kyle to tell him that I'd just left the house. He didn't want to, but I insisted. I forced my son to lie for me. What kind of father am I anyway? I'm teaching my son that I'm a liar and that he should lie."

Bob: "What price have you been paying for lying to Becky and Kyle?"

John: "I've probably made them mistrust me. Who can

blame them? I feel like apologizing."

Bob: "What would it take for you to admit that you lied to them and then apologize?"

John: "Courage."

Bob: "Well, what do you think? By apologizing you get to wipe the slate clean and start over."

John: "I'd have to start with Becky. She's confronted me a few times when I've lied, but I always denied it. It's time to come clean with her, I guess. I'm not sure I can tell my son because I don't think he's old enough to understand."

Bob: "Start with Becky, but you're wrong about your son. He understands. At least apologize for making him lie for you and tell him you'll never do it again. Then in the future, when you tell him you'll be at his school for an event, arrange your life to be there. Learn to keep your word, and he'll grow to trust you again. People who keep their word keep their relationships working."

John: "I'll apologize tonight. We'll see how it goes."

Bob: "Let me know."

The next time we met, John shared what happened when he apologized to Becky. She broke down crying. His apology made her see that he was making a change, which gave her hope that their relationship would get better. Kyle told his dad that he hated having to lie for him, so he was glad he wouldn't have to do it again.

COACHING TIPS

- Instead of lying automatically, make a more conscious choice. Maybe you'll choose to lie to make someone feel good or when you need to protect yourself and your loved ones, but you can quit lying to cover your ass.
- Instead of creating mistrust in your relationships by lying, work for trust by telling the truth and by keeping your word. When you do, you'll feel better about yourself and your relationships will improve.
- Don't say and do things you know you'll want to lie about. By living more cleanly, you'll be happier.
- Don't forget that the "golden thread" that makes relationships work well is trust, and telling the truth and keeping your word is what strengthens it.

CHAPTER 13

Feeling Red With Envy

*"I used to envy women who were beautiful,
but I got over that when I reached middle age.
Now I envy anyone with knees that work."*
Susan, a former long-distance runner

Envy is more common than most of us want to admit. It sneaks into our lives as thoughts about wanting what others have, like lots of money, power, the right job, good looks, a great body, a good marriage, successful children, peace of mind, and knees that work. Does it make us happy to think about the things we don't have that other people have in abundance? Of course not; it makes us miserable. We do it because we're machines running on automatic.

"Feeling red with envy" as a cause of unhappiness boils down to five thoughts people have without being fully aware of them. The red symbolizes the anger they sometimes feel toward those who have what they wish they had. The five thoughts are:

- I want what you've got
- I dislike you for having what you've got
- I dislike myself for disliking you for having what you've got
- I'm not satisfied with what I've got
- I dislike myself for not being satisfied with what I've got

I've worked with people who have envied others for their good looks, their wealth, and their luck having jobs they wish they had. Then there was Ted. For him, life was like watching commercials on TV, showing all the great products that he couldn't afford to buy. Imagine his frustration at seeing everyone have what he wanted. The day envy emerged as one of Ted's issues, I met him at the door wearing a bright yellow sweatshirt with a big smile printed on the front. Underneath the smile were the words, "Make your mind into a ray of sunshine."

Ted: "One of your creations, Dr. Bob?"

Bob: "Grand, isn't it? Did you know that unhappiness is the ability to miss seeing the humorous side of things? Without a sense of humor, achieving unhappiness is as easy as burning toast."

Ted: "When I least expect it, misery creeps in to mess up my day. It's hard to have a sense of humor about unhappiness because it seems to be such a serious problem."

Bob: "If a college had a graduate degree in unhappiness, there would be a seminar called 'How to wipe that smile off your face.' Another would be 'Living in the dark thinking it's the light.' When you received your Ph.Eu. Degree (Doctor of Extreme Unhappiness), you'd have a choice between two T-

CHAPTER 13

Feeling Red With Envy

shirts, one with an image of Darth Vader from Star Wars that says, "Don't bother me with humor because I've joined the dark side of the force." The other would say, "I'm an unhappiness machine. Don't oil me with humor."

Ted wasn't amused by my humor, so I got down to business.

Bob: "What do you want to work on today?"

Ted: "I was talking to a friend the other day about envy and how much misery it creates. Since then I've been catching myself feeling envy about all kinds of things, like people's personalities, their popularity, their intelligence, and, of course, their good looks. I've been down on myself for being so envious of others. It seems like a big defect."

Bob: "Any other kinds of envy that have you by the throat?"

Ted: "I know I envy people who find it easy to be happy. In fact, I found myself feeling a touch of anger toward people I saw last week with genuinely happy smiles."

Bob: "How about looking at your envy with a twist of humor?"

Ted: "Envy isn't funny."

Bob: "What about making it funny?"

Ted: "Hmm, let me think. Wouldn't it be funny to say to someone who has the nose you'd like, 'I want your nose!' Seeing the humorous side of envy, it's obvious that it's all about greed because most people have enough to be happy, including a nose that works."

Bob: "Have you ever thought about the fact that, by being unhappy, you reduce the envy others can feel toward you? Wouldn't it be great to have people envy you for being happy? Imagine being at the gates of heaven where a being of light asks you, 'Did other people envy you for being happy?' What would you say?"

Ted: "I'd have to say 'No.'"

Bob: "Hearing your answer, the being of light would say, 'Go back and try harder.'"

Ted: "I guess I will have to try harder."

Bob: "I know you had a hard week, but don't give up. I can see you changing. For the next week, when you catch yourself envying someone, take a moment to appreciate something you already have, like a nose that works. Being thankful for what you have will make you happier in a hurry."

Ted: "It's good to get some encouragement. Changing is hard. You think you have it and it slips away. It's like climbing a ladder where you go up three rungs and come down two."

Bob: "Ah, but notice that you're gaining a step each time."

Ted: "I guess that is progress."

Bob: "To keep you moving upward, I have something for you to use. I have this idea that one minute of coaching is all people need to be happier. Imagine showing up for a one-minute session with me that only costs one buck."

Ted: "I'd pay more if it works. How does it go?"

Bob: "I would say to you, 'You have one minute to get this. All you have to do is to listen and wake yourself up. This method for achieving happiness is called "the five quits." Quit blaming others for your problems and take responsibility for creating them yourself. Quit thinking you're helpless to solve those problems and get into action now. Quit believing the negative thoughts you have about yourself are true. Make up positive thoughts. Quit envying others for what they have and appreciate what you have. Quit thinking about your problems all the time and do something for someone who has bigger problems than you do. Those are "the five quits." Practice them and change your life. That's it.' You hand over your buck and walk out a bit stunned. Yet there's a part of you that's saying, 'Hey that made sense!'"

Ted: "If I practiced 'the five quits,' I'd be happier in a

CHAPTER 13　　　　　　　　　　Feeling Red With Envy

week. In fact, if I just stop envying others, I'll create a nice change."

Bob: "When you stop envying others, you'll begin to see more abundance in your life. Seeing each day as an opportunity to give thanks for what you have, you'll feel lucky to have so many blessings. Feeling that lucky will make you happier."

Ted: "Bob, this has been a great session. I'm going to practice 'the five quits' and focus on feeling lucky."

I've always been fascinated by the fact that so few people, with Ted as an exception, pause to notice how envy sneaks into their thinking to make them unhappy. Being blind to envy is probably a survival mechanism. If too much truth is faced, people might blow up. Ted, on the other hand, was determined to turn off his envy machine. He did this in a clever way. He put up on his kitchen wall a large piece of paper divided into two columns. In the first column, he recorded his envies. In the second, he noted something he was thankful for at that moment. This practice helped him transform envy into giving thanks.

COACHING TIPS

- Watch how often envy sneaks into your thinking to make you discontented.
- Notice how you dislike, maybe even hate, the people who have what you want.
- Instead of envying them, be thankful for what you have.
- Before going to sleep at night, become aware of one thing for which you're thankful. Before getting up in the morning, do the same thing. Make thankfulness a thought you have often during any given day. Practicing thankfulness will increase your happiness.

- To increase your happiness in a hurry, practice "the five quits."

Creative Sidetrack

Going into debt to buy what we envy others for having is another source of unhappiness. My life is a case in point. One day, I began thinking in earnest about my TV set. I wasn't appreciating it. I was thinking about how small it was because the screen is only nineteen inches. When I saw how big my friends' TV sets were, I had to fight off an attack of envy.

One afternoon, when envy and discontent teamed up against me, I decided to go shopping for a TV. As I walked around the store looking at all the great sets, I felt my desire grow. "You want one of those super big ones," a voice in me insisted. When I hesitated, it shouted, "Quit stalling and get the damn thing! It's going to make you a happy man!"

I started narrowing down my many choices until I pinpointed the one I wanted. I knew I'd have to go further into debt to buy it because it was top of the line. How I'd pay for it fell away as an issue as my urgency to buy it grew. Just as I was at the point of deciding to get it, I heard a faint voice in me whisper, "Bob, do you really, really, really need this?"

I started off my TV shopping trip knowing that I

desperately needed a new TV. All my friends had the fancy new models, some as big as a wall. But, did I really, really, really need one? No! With this realization, a light went on in my mind and I left the store. I didn't even look back. The good news is that I didn't go further into debt, and my nineteen-inch TV is still working fine. So what did I learn from this? When I'm in the grip of a desire for something to buy, I ask myself, "Do I really, really, really need this?" Most of the time, the answer is "No!"

Think of something you want to buy because you know you need it, then give it the consumer truth test.

Do I really, really, really need this?

CHAPTER 14

Resistance Just Makes You More Miserable

*"I'm very creative, but in a sick kind of way.
When I look outside in the morning and see gloomy weather,
I make up my mind that it's going to be a lousy day,
and by the time I get to work it is."*
Jan, office manager

Resisting what we can't change is probably the most compelling proof that human beings are stupid. Yet we do it all the time. We resist the weather when it doesn't suit us, long traffic lines, red lights when we're in a hurry, and work we have to do that's unpleasant, like writing reports, cleaning the house, and taking out the garbage. Resistance to the way life occurs is a major source of unhappiness for most people, and they don't know it. They beat themselves up when they could stop resisting and embrace reality.

Susan was a big resister who struggled with her roller-coaster life, sometimes going to the heights of joy and then falling into valleys of despair. I had given her an assignment at the end of our last session, so I was interested to know what she had done with it.

Bob: "You were going to keep track of things that made you unhappy last week. What did you come up with?"

Susan: "Well, I became upset last Saturday when I had what I thought was a fifteen-minute job to do and it took three hours. Last Monday, I got angry when a guy who was supposed to meet me for lunch was twenty minutes late. Last night, I was disappointed when my favorite TV program was bumped by a special. As I looked at myself in your mirror coming in just now, I didn't like how my hair looked. I hate my red, curly hair. I've always wished that I had straight brown hair. It's been a hell of a week, and this is taking into account only the garbage piled up to my shoelaces."

Bob: "Was it different from other weeks?"

Susan: "No, about the same."

Bob: "I'm reminded of a quote I saw recently. 'Moments of happiness are the small punctuation marks that give us a chance to breathe between the long phrases of misery.' Would you agree?"

Susan: "I'd say being miserable is what people seem to do best, which is why they do so much of it."

Bob: "I'm going to tell you something that will probably surprise you. Your mind is full of file cabinets. Do you know what's stored in them?"

Susan: "I have no idea."

Bob: "They are loaded with all your desires and expectations. You have desires and expectations covering how you should look, how people should treat you, and how you should behave at weddings, dinner parties, and while giving a

CHAPTER 14 — Resistance Just Makes You More Miserable

speech. Your desires and expectations are sources of a huge amount of misery."

Susan: "What do you mean?"

Bob: "When life occurs in opposition to a desire or expectation, you'll become frustrated, probably angry, and definitely unhappy. For example, when you started the project at home, you expected it to take fifteen minutes. When it took three hours, you became angry. For years, you've been resisting having red, curly hair, but you can't change what nature gave you. In each of the situations you mentioned earlier, you had no power to make a change, yet you put up resistance and suffered from it. Is this making sense?"

Susan: "So you're saying that by resisting what I can't change, I'm setting myself up to suffer. That seems stupid, doesn't it?"

Bob: "What we can change, we should try to change. What we can't change, we should accept. As a practice, 'no resistance' will take away your unhappiness faster than a belly laugh takes away the blues."

Quietly, then picking up volume, the carefree sounds of a waltz filled the house.

Susan: "Do you hear that music?"

Bob: "Yeah, I hear it. My place is full of the spirits of famous people, so I think someone's coming. Just be open to what happens."

In the next second, Fred Astaire, the legendary dancing star of movie fame, waltzed into the room. After a few turns around the study, he sat down beside Susan on the couch.

Fred: "Look, Susan, life won't go your way all the time. Instead of wrestling with it, dance with it. Banging your head against a wall without knowing you're doing it is ignorance. Discovering what you're doing and then continuing to do it is stupidity. Learning to dance with the circumstances you can't change is smart. Being smart will make you happier."

Having said his piece, Fred got up and waltzed out of the room while Susan and I watched in amazement.

Bob: "Fred has given you something to work on next week. See if you can dance with what you can't change."

Susan: "Being stupid has been so easy for me that giving up resistance to what I can't change scares me a bit. How am I going to handle being that smart?"

Bob: "I'll bet you'll get used to it."

I walked Susan to the front door. She stopped at the mirror and said, "Red, curly hair, I accept you!" Susan had gotten the coaching.

When Susan and I finished our work together about a month later, she was still practicing no resistance. She told me, "I keep catching myself resisting what I can't change and suffering from it. I can't believe how much I do this! Yet I'm getting better at catching myself. As soon as I realize that I'm resisting, I can stop it fairly easily if I remember my practice. 'Susan, wake up, stupid, and dance with it!'"

COACHING TIPS

- Notice when you're resisting what you can't change and how your resistance makes you frustrated and unhappy.
- Follow Fred's advice to dance with the circumstances you can't change instead of resisting them.
- When you've quit resisting, look for opportunities to deal with reality in new ways. For example, instead of getting frustrated while you're waiting at a traffic light, use the time to count your blessings.

CHAPTER 15

Visiting Your Tombstone

*"I once lost sleep over the most insignificant things.
Now I'm an insignificant thing who's asleep."*
Tombstone epitaph

There's no quicker way to reduce the size of a problem than by visiting a cemetery. Walking among the tombstones gives us a broader perspective, which makes it easier to shrink any "large" problem down to its proper size. What are a few of the little problems that we make bigger than they really are?

- Having a nose that's too big or too small
- Being too tall or too short
- Losing a game
- Getting caught making a mistake
- Breaking up with someone
- Getting older

- When we're older, developing wrinkles

Mimi was waiting tables at a café when we started working together. She had a delicate appearance, a fiery and creative spirit, and the magical ability to transform even the smallest problem into a Class Five tornado. As a result, she lived a dramatic soap-opera life. While that kind of life created a lot of excitement for her, it also served up a fair amount of suffering. One day, I selected one of my creations to wear with the idea of nudging her closer to wake-up time. The words on the front were, "Soap-opera lives are fun to watch, but hard to live in."

Mimi: "Did you wear that shirt for my benefit?"

Bob: "I was thinking about you. Shakespeare would have loved you because your life is one tragedy after another. In fact, I think he would have learned something from you. When are you going to stop living the soap-opera life?"

Mimi: "It's funny you'd say that. Yesterday, one of my girlfriends got so angry at me she stomped out of the room, turning at the last moment to yell, 'You are the world's biggest drama queen!' At first I was angry and hurt but, within the hour, I had to admit she was right. I get upset over the littlest things. High drama is my game."

Bob: "Give me an example."

Mimi: "Just this morning, I served a guy at the café two soft-boiled eggs, and he told me to take them back because they were overdone. That really pissed me off. They were perfectly nice eggs! I made a big deal about it in the kitchen."

Bob: "Anything else?"

Mimi: "Let's see. Last weekend, I lost my temper when my puppy pooped on the carpet."

Bob: "I have an idea. Let's think about which of those problems would end up on your tombstone."

Mimi: "It's funny when you think of it that way. Imagine a tombstone that says, 'My puppy pooped on my carpet.'"

CHAPTER 15

Visiting Your Tombstone

Bob: "I remember when Johnny Carson of TV fame was asked what he would have inscribed on his tombstone. He said, 'Be right back'. What would your inscription read?"

Mimi: "'Now I don't need to worry about becoming happier any more.' That's what I'd have inscribed."

Bob: "That's pretty negative, isn't it? You have to die to escape from worrying about whether you'll become happier?"

Mimi: "Oh-oh. I just stepped in it."

Bob: "Let's try to get you out of it. What's your biggest problem?"

Mimi: "Struggling to be happier."

Bob: "Try again."

Mimi: "That isn't it?"

Bob: "No, it isn't. But it's related."

Mimi: "If struggling to be happier isn't the big problem, what is? I'm starting to feel that I'm on a quiz show, and I've have just been asked the million-dollar question. If I don't get the right answer, I'm screwed, which means I've lost big bucks. Can you give me a hint?"

Bob: "It's something you're afraid of."

Mimi: "Hmm, what am I afraid of that is bigger than struggling to be happier?"

She closed her eyes to seek an answer, so I waited, hoping she'd find a good one. After a few minutes, it was clear that she'd seen something.

Mimi: "When I closed my eyes, I imagined Mr. Spock of Star Trek standing in front of me. I laid out the issue for him. I felt him reading the deeper parts of my mind. In a few seconds, he said, 'I have the answer. The bigger problem than struggling to be happier is your belief that you will never succeed.' I said to him, 'You're right! It's my belief that I won't change enough, that I can't reach the level of happiness I want! Instead, I'll spend the rest of my life wallowing in misery.' Then, I saw my tombstone. It was inscribed with the words, 'I didn't attain enough happiness because, fearing I couldn't, I didn't really try. Don't make the same mistake'. Now I know what the bigger problem is. I lack confidence in my ability to change. I feel that I'll never be able to achieve the level of happiness I'm after."

Bob: "You believe that you're a loser, is that it?"

Mimi: "I expect to be over the long haul. I don't think I'm capable of becoming the happy person I want to be. I lack the confidence to succeed."

Bob: "If you lived in that fearful thought for the rest of your life, what would happen?"

Mimi: "I guess I'd stay stuck where I am and never change."

Bob: "Lots of people do that, so it is a choice for you. What do you think?"

Mimi: "Be more miserable than I want to be? I don't think so."

Humphrey Bogart was listening to this whole thing and couldn't contain himself any longer. Catching us by surprise, he stepped out of the shadows, pulled Mimi up from the couch and gave her a big hug. Then he said to her, "You have the power to change, can't ya see it? All you have to do is keep working at it, like quit being lazy and get into action. Look, you're not always going to be happy, but you can be a lot happier than ya are. Quit whining and get moving. Life isn't for chickens. Hey, when I was young, I couldn't hug nobody. It just wasn't in me, but look at what I just done. I hugged ya 'cause I changed. If I can hug ya, you can become happier. Are you willing? Do we have a deal?"

Mimi: "Okay. We have a deal."

With a commitment from Mimi, Bogart stepped back into the shadows.

Bob: "That was an amazing encounter! Bogart did some great coaching and you got it. You just convinced yourself that you have the potential to become happier. Live in that thought for the rest of your life and your tombstone will read, 'More

CHAPTER 15 — *Visiting Your Tombstone*

happiness was achieved than I thought possible, but it took some sweat.'"

Mimi: "Like Bogart said, it's up to me to create happiness in my life. This was an important session. Now I understand why his photo is the largest in the room. Bogart's the king of action."

Bob: "No doubt about it. Become more like him and see how much happiness you can create."

When I saw Mimi again, she told me that she had purchased a large photograph of Bogart to hang in her front room. His presence reminded her to keep working for happiness even in the face of setbacks.

COACHING TIPS

- Be aware of the times when you make your problems much bigger than they really are and how much extra weight you have to carry as a consequence. Notice how, by making your problems bigger, you make living harder.
- When you catch yourself exaggerating the importance of a problem, ask yourself whether it will make it onto your tombstone. If you know it won't, then reduce the size of the problem in your mind so you can deal with it more effectively.
- Keep working to create happiness in your life. To stay in action, remember the tombstone inscription that says, "More happiness was achieved than I thought possible, but it took some sweat."

Creative Sidetrack

At this point you might be thinking. "This self-awareness stuff is exhausting," so maybe it's time for a sidetrack to give you a breather. I'm using "breather" on purpose. Have you ever thought about the fact that you are a "breather?"

For a few moments, focus on your breathing.

Good news! You're alive!

Take a moment to appreciate being alive.

Good news! You're one of a kind! There will never be another person like you in the universe, ever. When you were born, you were already special.

Take a moment to reflect on your uniqueness.

Good news! You've already made a difference!

Take a moment to consider what wouldn't exist if you had never been born.

CHAPTER 16

Finding Your Inner Wisdom

*"I seldom hear people talk about wisdom,
yet it's as precious as love."*
Elizabeth, writer

A woman in her eighties with a wealth of experience told me, "Wisdom is just being smart about all the things we're normally stupid about." I just loved how down-to-earth her understanding was and how useful. This is in contrast to the popular idea that wisdom is rare and only a few people have it. If we accept that idea, it's easy to convince ourselves that we're not one of the few. By believing that we're not wise, it never dawns on us to ask, "What's the wise thing to think or do here?" When we omit this question, we fail to encourage our minds to seek wisdom, which is quite stupid.

Let me tell you a wisdom story about Dan, a talented long-distance runner in his prime.

I learned during our first meeting that he had a problem he needed to resolve as a runner. He told me he wanted so badly to win that he sometimes over-trained, which caused injuries, and during a race he started out strong but often fell back at the end. The day I'll describe was a turning point for him. It was a time full of magic and the miraculous.

When I met Dan at the door that day, I told him there was a special guest waiting to see him.

When we walked into my study, an old Asian man was sitting on the couch. He had long hair and a thin beard of silky white. His clothing was simple, like a peasant's from long ago. I motioned for Dan to sit beside him. Dan sat down and looked over at me, hoping I'd say something. I didn't. The tension in the room mounted because this old man—a great sage—was in our presence.

Dan: "This silence is killing me. Hello. I'm Dan. Who are you?"

Lao-tzu: "People call me Lao-tzu."

Dan: "You're kidding! You've been dead for centuries. I've heard about you because you were the sage who created Taoism."

Lao-tzu: "There were others who contributed."

Dan: "What are you doing here?"

Lao-tzu: "Bob asked me to come. He told me you had a problem that needed wisdom."

Bob: "Dan, I told Lao-tzu how you've been unhappy because you've been failing to live up to your potential as a runner. I thought he might help."

Dan: "I've devoted my life to running. I know I can run smarter and faster than I've been running. I'm capable of breaking records, but I struggle with injuries and can't seem to win. I really want to win."

Lao-tzu: "Why are you so ambitious?"

Dan: "If I didn't have the ambition to win and want to

CHAPTER 16

Finding Your Inner Wisdom

win badly, I'd lose my motivation to run. I can't see how that would help me."

Lao-tzu: "It is because you fail to see how being extreme works against you."

Dan: "I don't get what you mean."

Lao-tzu: "Anything you do that becomes extreme will work against you. It can be trying too hard to win, trying too hard to impress others, trying too hard to be famous. The opposite is also a big problem, when you fail to try hard enough. When running, try but not too hard."

Dan: "I don't see how that will help me."

Lao-tzu: "When you try too hard, what happens?"

Dan: "Sometimes I train harder than I should and injure myself."

Lao-tzu: "Ah, so trying too hard makes you tighten up. Is that true?"

Dan: "In a sense, I guess it does."

Lao-tzu: "When you fail to try hard enough, what happens?"

Dan: "I tend to give up. There are times when I'm racing, especially when I'm falling behind, that I lose my will to run."

Lao-tzu: "Can you see that you run with two fears in hand? One is the fear that you will fail. The other is the fear that you will give up."

Dan: "I guess you're right. So what's a better way for me?"

Lao-tzu: "Tao arises when you balance the opposing sides of yourself. Not too far one way. Not too far the other way. In the middle is just right. It is where balance lives. Balance is where happiness is born. As a runner, try hard but not so hard that it works against you. As you discover the beautiful midpoint between wanting to win and accepting defeat, you will relax. Being relaxed will liberate your energy. Instead of giving up, you will have enough energy to keep going."

Dan: "You're saying that I should try to win but be willing to lose. When I can accept defeat, I'll run in a more relaxed way. Maybe I'll be freer to enjoy running because I won't be as afraid of losing and giving up."

Lao-tzu: "Ah, you are coming to wisdom. Yes, focus as much on your love of running as your love of winning. Balance will serve you as a runner and in many realms of life. Dan, you are of two minds about everything. All the opposites reside in your nature. You can be funny and serious, rigid and flexible, engaged and aloof, hardworking and lazy. Duality is who you are. Once you understand your dual nature, notice where you are living out of balance. Are you doing something too much or too little? Do you talk too much or too little? Do you control too much or too little? Are your life commitments too heavy or too light?"

Dan: "So what do I do when I see that I'm being too extreme?"

Lao-tzu: "When you see where you are out of balance, correct it by moving in the opposite direction. If you have too many commitments, cut back so you can enjoy life. If you talk too much, practice listening. If you are too quiet, practice speaking. If you are too rigid, practice being flexible. If you seek praise too much, practice being humble."

Dan: "What a simple but amazing view of life! By seeking balance, I'll create a new way to run and a new way to live. Thank you, Lao-tzu, for enlightening me."

Lao-tzu: "Dan, you have been a very good student."

Dan and I watched as Lao-tzu got up, bowed with respect, and then disappeared through the west wall.

Bob: "Dan, now you see how wisdom arises from being in balance and living a balanced life. I think Lao-tzu would call balance 'the secret passageway to happiness.'"

Dan: "I don't know what to say, except that I'm a bit overwhelmed by today's discoveries. Lao-tzu is a great teacher.

CHAPTER 16   *Finding Your Inner Wisdom*

Thanks for inviting him."

Bob: "You're welcome. I always enjoy having him come because he reminds me about the connection between balance and wisdom. When you can ride your life without falling over, you will know that you have created a balanced mind and a balanced life."

Dan learned from this session that his problem with running was not the real issue. It was a symptom of living out of balance in other ways. Lao-tzu's wisdom about balance made its way into many parts of Dan's life, affecting his relationships and his sense of self. In time, he found a way to be balanced in himself, so his life worked better. As a result, he became a happier man. Incidentally, he also liberated himself for running and broke some of the records he sought.

COACHING TIPS

- Know that you are of two minds about everything. All the opposites reside in your nature. To achieve greater wisdom, create more balance in yourself and your life. Do you talk too much or too little? Control too much or too little? Are your commitments too heavy or too light? When you see where you are out of balance, correct it by moving in the opposing direction until you find the midpoint between the opposites. When you do, you will have created "just right."
- When you can ride your life without falling over, you will have achieved a more balanced mind and life. In greater balance, you'll be a happier person.

CHAPTER 17

Putting A New Spin On Your Life

"Life is empty until we fill it up with meaning."
Robert, nurse

I stopped at a traffic light one day and my eye caught a bumper sticker on the car ahead. It said, "If you don't know where you're going, you won't get there." One thing that makes people unhappy is that they don't know where they're going. They don't have a clear understanding of their life purposes. Without a clear sense of purpose, their lives can feel empty and meaningless. At some point in my work with people, I ask them about their life purposes. Most don't know what I mean because they've never thought about it. By declaring their purposes, they realize why they were born and what they were meant to do. Once they know their life purposes, they quickly develop the power to create lives with direction and meaning.

When Jackie met with me the first time, she was an

emotional wreck. She suffered from low self-esteem, which meant she was constantly under attack from her inner judge. She was miserable a good part of the time but, as we worked together, she began to see what was making her unhappy and slowly corrected it—mainly by changing how she thought about herself and life. It was inspiring to watch her change. I still remember the stark contrast between my first meeting with her and our last time together. It was a session that affected me deeply because Jackie coached me.

Jackie: "I need to tell you something now, or I might change my mind. I've decided to stop our work together and get on with my life. I'm at a point where I want to be responsible for the adventure of becoming happier. Now I know that life's never going to be a smooth sea. It's going to have all kinds of turbulence thrown in. I've learned a lot from you. You've given me tools that I'll be able to use for the rest of my life."

Bob: "Wonderful! It feels great to see you preparing to play the game of life on your own. It's one of the most interesting and challenging games there is."

Jackie: "To prepare myself to play, there's one more thing I'd like to cover."

Bob: "What's that?"

Jackie: "I want to talk about what I should be doing with my life."

Bob: "What would you like to do?"

Jackie: "I've been waiting for a sign but haven't been getting anything."

Bob: "Why wait? Why don't you make up your own life purposes? Life purposes are what we decide to create so our lives have much clearer direction, more meaning, and greater uniqueness. It's like declaring what we were born to do. What are a few things you'd like to create as life purposes?"

Jackie: "So that's like putting a new spin on my life?"

Bob: "Something like that."

CHAPTER 17 — Putting A New Spin On Your Life

Jackie: "I think to be more generous would be one purpose, especially being kind and showing more appreciation for others, my life, and myself. That part of our work together made a big difference to me. So did stopping my put-downs."

Bob: "Declaring that purpose should make you happier. What other purposes would you like to create?"

Jackie: "I'd like to be more playful. I want more light to come out of me to balance my darker side."

Bob: "Playfulness is important. It's the creative spirit in us seeking to have a bit of fun. What about a third purpose?"

Jackie: "I think it will have something to do with helping other people become happier. I've realized that being resigned to unhappiness the way I was for years is not a good way to live. I'm not sure how I'll help yet, but I will. I'll also work for more happiness within myself."

Bob: "Anything else?"

Jackie: "There is something, but I hesitate to say it. I want to create more love in the world. This is the boldest claim I've ever made, but since I know I'm not going to live forever, why not be bold? I'll do my best to be a source of love for everyone."

Bob: "That's a very compelling purpose, but there's something about being a source of love for everyone that's so lofty, it seems unrealistic."

Jackie got up from the couch, pulled me up from my chair, and gave me a hug. Caught off guard, I felt awkward and embarrassed. I gave her a quick hug and then pushed her gently away.

Jackie: "Dr. Bob, you've taught me a lot. Now maybe I can offer you something in return. As you pushed me away, I wondered whether you're afraid of extending your love out into the world. I am, too. Probably everyone is."

I walked to the window and looked into my garden. Standing there, I felt sad and disappointed in myself. My eyes filled with tears. Jackie had cut into the truth about me and was waking me up. It was an awkward, yet beautiful, moment. When I sat back down again, I felt raw.

Jackie: "Are you all right?"

Bob: "What you said hit me because it's true. I have no problem loving people in my close circle of family and friends, but the thought of loving people outside that circle scares me. It makes me think about the saints of the great religions. They allowed themselves to be devoured by love, compassion, and service for others. I know there's a part of me that wants to be a source of love for everyone like those saints, but I hold back."

Jackie: "You've been a source of love for me, and it's helped me in more ways than I can say. Being a happiness coach who helps people overcome their misery is an example of loving at its best."

Bob: "Being a source of love for people I don't know is the big challenge for me. If I loved them, I'd feel obligated to help them. I resist doing that because it would force me to make sacrifices I'm unwilling to make. It would throw my life out of balance. Going from loving blood relatives to loving species relatives is too big a leap for me. I'm not cut out to be a saint. I accept that, but with a twinge of guilt for not loving others enough."

Jackie: "I feel the same way. I hold back from loving, too. The thought of it scares me because of the obligations. I would feel called upon to respond to the needs of the poor right now, not tomorrow. Bob, is there a different approach to this problem?"

Bob: "You've been consulting your inner wise woman when you need guidance. What would she say?"

Jackie: "I think she'd say, 'Don't go overboard in either direction. Love as much as you can without driving yourself nuts. Seek the middle way, even when you're being a source of love for humanity.' As I think about it, I believe that she'd urge us to concentrate on liking rather than loving, because liking is

CHAPTER 17 Putting A New Spin On Your Life

easier and doesn't make such heavy demands on us. I can hear her say, 'Liking is the middle way. It will produce the best results over time.' Does this make sense?"

Bob: "I can't believe how wise you're becoming. Liking ourselves and others is good enough. Using that as a starting point, we can help others as long as we also look out for ourselves. This gives us a balanced way to be helpful so we don't become so frustrated or guilty that we end up doing nothing. Jackie, I want you to know that I like you."

Jackie: "I like you, too. You know, if people could like themselves and others a bit more, things would change for the better. This makes me want to revise my last life purpose. Instead of being a source of love for everyone, I'll like myself and others, while still loving as much as I can. I'll balance helping others and looking out for myself. This will make my inner wise woman smile."

Bob: "It will make me smile, too."

Jackie: "Well, I got what I wanted today. Now I have four purposes that will help me shape my life."

We sat together in silence for a minute. We were hesitating to end the session because what had happened was priceless. It comes from life as a delicate gift that is rare and fleeting.

Bob: "Before you go, I want to give you a little gift as thanks for what you gave me today."

I went to my desk and drew out a paper I had written. Handing it to Jackie, I said, "I had fun creating this. I hope you enjoy it."

Jackie: "Thanks. 'Meeting the Almighty Coach'—what a funny title!"

Bob: "It might help you keep your happiness growing."

I'll never forget my last day with Jackie. In a short time, she created important life goals for herself and then, with honesty and kindness, she taught me something about myself.

COACHING TIPS

- Develop four life purposes in order to create more direction and meaning in your life.
- Help others become happier. Teaching the happiness principles you've learned will embed them in your heart and mind so you continue to develop as a person.
- Learn to like yourself and others, and love as much as you can.
- Make "How can I become a happier person?" the guiding question of your life. With that question in mind, always be reaching for happiness.

Creative Sidetrack

Some people think heaven is a place where we're judged for our good and bad deeds. Well, there's an alternative view. When you arrive at the borderland, a being of light will ask you one question, "Did you learn to like yourself?"

To prepare yourself to answer, identify at least four things you like about yourself.

Add at least four things you're going to learn to like about yourself.

Imagine liking yourself so much at the end of your life that, when the being of light asks the question, you respond with a resounding "Yes!"

Finally, think about what you will do now and in the future so you like yourself that much at the end. Be specific, so you'll know what you need to create.

Be inspired by a message I saw hanging in the hallway of a school: "Most people don't like themselves enough. Be one of the deviants."

CHAPTER 18

Meeting The Almighty Coach

"The quickest way to make someone mad is to challenge their beliefs. The quickest way to make them happy is to agree with them."
Susan, college teacher

One afternoon on a hilltop near town, I was doing some creative writing on my wireless laptop computer when huge billowing clouds suddenly appeared. A moment later, thunder rolled and a great wind came up. Amid the turbulence, I saw the Almighty Coach. I was stunned. Being near the Almighty Coach is an awe-inspiring and scary thing, but also a huge opportunity. How many people have the chance to be in the presence of such a compelling source of knowledge? With my hands sweating and heart pounding, I waited for something to happen.

From the cloud, a voice rumbled: "Hi, Dr. Bob. I've come to get your help."

Bob: "Who me? I'm just a measly happiness coach. Who am I to help the Almighty Coach?"

The Almighty Coach: "I know you're a happiness coach. That's why I need you. You see, a long time ago, I sent human beings the Ten Commandments, hoping that by obeying them they would learn to be good."

Bob: "From reading our newspapers, you'll see that we haven't been doing very well on the goodness scale."

The Almighty Coach: "Given what I've seen, I'd say about a five on a ten-point scale. With your assistance Bob, I'm going to lay down some principles to help humans become happier. If they increase their happiness even a little bit, I'll bet they'll find it easier to be good."

Bob: "Yeah, happiness can produce some great things."

The Almighty Coach: "Right! So let's get to work. Get your chisel and take two stone tablets from the stack I brought with me. I keep them handy in case humans ask me to make things up for them."

Bob: "You're really out of date, aren't you? People use computers for writing now, not slabs of stone. See, this is my laptop computer."

The Almighty Coach: "How can something so tiny hold the important words I'm about to speak? I've always thought stone tablets were an impressive way to present my ideas. They give my thoughts greater weight so humans will pay attention."

Bob: "Don't worry. Computers are great. Once I get your words down, I can send them to every e-mail list in the world. I hope your words aren't treated as spam or we'll have trouble."

The Almighty Coach: "Isn't spam something humans eat?"

Bob: "Yes, but this is different. It's what people send as e-mail messages, thinking they'll sell something, like products that keep women looking young forever or give men a chance to elevate themselves for thirty-six hours so their egos feel better."

CHAPTER 18　　　　　　　　　　　Meeting The Almighty Coach

The Almighty Coach: "Hey, if it makes them happy, I'm all for it. But maybe they're missing the bigger picture. We'll see that picture unfold as I lay out the commitments they need to keep to be happier. I want to be clear, so let me think for a few minutes."

Bob: "Take your time. This is big stuff."

The Almighty Coach (after thinking for a while): "Okay, I have the First Commitment!"

Bob: "What is it?"

The Almighty Coach: "You're going to like this one. 'Quit thinking in ways that force you to question your value, lead you to criticize yourself, and make you unhappy. Think in positive ways.'"

Bob: "That's too long. No one will remember it. I don't mean to be critical, but you should have made us smarter. Come up with something simpler so we can remember it."

The Almighty Coach: "Well, yes, here's a simpler way to put it. 'Quit beating yourself up with negative thoughts and stories. Make up positive ones.'"

Bob: "That's better." I went to work quickly, my fingers racing across the keyboard. "Okay. It's entered."

The Almighty Coach: "Hey, computers are a lot quicker than carving in stone! I love not having to wait so long! Even though I'm eternal, I still get impatient."

Bob: "What comes next?"

The Almighty Coach: "I have another great one for you. 'Instead of wallowing in your unhappiness about other people's success and disliking them for it, be thankful for what you have.'"

Bob: "That's too long again. If you keep doing this, we'll be here all day and I have an appointment to keep."

The Almighty Coach: "Okay. What do you think of this? 'Quit envying others. Appreciate what you have.'"

Bob: "You're the Almighty and All-Knowing One, so

whatever you say goes."

The Almighty Coach: "I love how humans believe those things about me because I can get away with a lot. If I were them, I'd bring me down a peg or two."

Bob: "No way! We need to believe you're all-powerful so we can feel secure in the knowledge that you will fulfill your role of taking care of us."

The Almighty Coach: "Am I supposed to take care of you? That's not in my contract. In my contract, it just says 'Be.'"

Bob: "It's no wonder that we get disappointed in you at times, especially when the world is being shredded and you do nothing to stop it."

The Almighty Coach: "I gave you a bigger brain to solve your own problems. Why should I meddle in your affairs? It would take away your challenges so your brain would quit evolving. Remember, I meant for humans to evolve, although I expected you to change at a much faster pace."

Bob: "This is interesting stuff, but we need to go on with the commitments." In a flash, 'Quit envying others; appreciate what you have,' was in my computer. "Okay, I have that one down."

The Almighty Coach: "Good, because I've got a doozy. I'll keep it short. 'Quit working so hard to prove yourself. Accept and like yourself as you are.'"

Bob: "I love this commitment because everyone is trying to prove their value so they'll be admired and successful. If they took all the energy they put into impressing others into learning to accept and like themselves, they'd become happier in a hurry." I quickly typed out the new commitment while I was muttering, "This is a great one."

The Almighty Coach: "I'm learning a lot from this session. Let's see. What comes next? Ah, I've got it. 'Stop being so stupid.'"

Bob: "That's unclear. Be more specific."

CHAPTER 18

Meeting The Almighty Coach

The Almighty Coach: "What I mean is that people are always fighting against what they can't change so they make themselves and others unhappy. It's stupid, wouldn't you say?"

Bob: "No doubt about it, but make it clearer. What do you think of this? 'Quit being stupid by resisting what you can't change. Be smart by accepting it.'"

The Almighty Coach: "Hey, that's good. I like how you juxtapose stupid and smart. It shows that I don't know everything. In fact, sometimes I'm convinced I don't know anything. When I'm feeling that way, I tune in my radio to your religious services to hear that I know everything. That always gives me a boost."

Bob: "Okay. Let's see. We're ready for the Fifth Commitment."

The Almighty Coach: "'Quit getting lost in self-pity. Do something for others who have bigger problems than you.' How's that for the next one?"

Bob: "That's going to be a tough one because getting, rather than giving, seems to be what many people do best. Yet I like the direction you're encouraging us to take. I just wouldn't bet on the results."

The Almighty Coach: "I know getting is easier than giving for humans. I wish they were more generous, but they don't listen to me when I offer suggestions. If they admitted the truth, they'd see how much they resist my guidance because they relate to me as a super-parent. This idea works against me because of their urge to defy their parents. Luckily, they fear me a lot more than their parents so they're more willing to toe the lines I lay down. They created the belief that I'm all-powerful so they would have to behave better. Unfortunately, that belief is weakening so my influence is declining. If that keeps up, who knows how badly they'll behave?"

Bob: "That's an overly pessimistic view."

The Almighty Coach: "I'll leave the optimism to those

131

people on earth. I think you call them 'liberals.'"

Bob: "I'm a liberal."

The Almighty Coach: "You must be disappointed a lot."

Bob: "I see your point." In short order, I had the new commitment in my computer.

The Almighty Coach: "I'm ready with the next one. 'Quit treating yourself and others badly. Treat yourself and others well.' You notice I'm not saying be honest, kind, respectful, appreciative, and accepting of yourself and others. When things become too concrete, humans will be clearer about how to disobey me. Make it general and then they won't know what to do except behave themselves."

Bob: "I hope I can persuade people to honor this commitment. It would make everyone happier." As I typed, I noticed the Almighty Coach growing impatient and excited.

The Almighty Coach: "Wait till you hear this one! 'Quit whining about being unhappy. To be happy, create a positive attitude.'"

Bob: "I thought some of your other commitments were difficult, but this one is really tough. I think people just don't like to change. They'd rather talk about it than do it."

The Almighty Coach: "I can't blame them. I don't like to change either. Recently, one of my assistants suggested a new positioning of angels among the clouds. I refused. Hey, I'm accustomed to seeing them where they've been playing their harps for eons. I can understand why people don't want to change. They get used to things as they are, even when they're miserable. Known misery is often much more appealing than unknown possibilities, right?"

Bob: "Okay, I have this one finished. What's next?"

The Almighty Coach: "Here's another one. 'Quit making your problems so big. Notice how small they really are.' Humans make themselves miserable by thinking their problems are big when they aren't. If they had my problems, they'd know

CHAPTER 18

Meeting The Almighty Coach

what 'big' means. Hey, I'm running the universe! You have no idea of the number of species I have to manage on the billions of planets in my domain. What humans need to understand is that they're not the big cheese, but just a faint, cheesy aroma that catches my attention from time to time."

Bob: "It sounds like you have a horrendous job!"

The Almighty Coach: "I've got so much to do, I mess up a lot. However, through time, everything goes to the average so, overall, I do okay."

Bob: "I have the last commitment down. What's next?"

The Almighty Coach: "Here's the next one. 'Quit being so one-sided. Create more balance within yourself.' When humans learn to live in greater balance, they won't be so upset about being unhappy from time to time. Sure, they should seek to be happy because unhappiness makes them miserable, but there will be times when it's fine to be unhappy. See, there are two kinds of unhappiness: the kind humans make up to torture themselves, like how they suffer from putting themselves down; and unhappiness caused by the nature of life, such as loss, disappointment, and breakups. You know what I mean. If people got rid of the former, their legitimate unhappiness wouldn't be so hard to bear."

Bob: "Balance seems to be the key to a happier life, but it's really difficult to achieve! I only know a few people who are even interested in it." I hurried to get this commitment down because it was getting late. "Well, that does it! Are we finished?"

The Almighty Coach: "No. There is one more very important commitment! 'Quit thinking your exaggerated fears are true. Shrink them down to fit in the palm of your hand.'"

Bob: "I'm glad you didn't forget that one because our exaggerated fears hold us back and make us unhappy." My fingers flew across the keyboard as I quickly typed in the new commitment.

The Almighty Coach: "Okay. Let's stop here. If you give

humans too much to think about, they become confused and forget everything. So how many commitments did we end up with?"

Bob: "Can you believe that you've come up with Ten Commitments? What's this thing you have about ten?"

The Almighty Coach: "Don't ask me. I don't know everything."

Bob: "I think your Ten Commitments are wonderful! If people keep them, they'll become a lot happier. However, I have a concern."

The Almighty Coach: "That doesn't surprise me because humans are full of concerns, which is why they never have peace of mind. What's your concern?"

Bob: "I think people will keep your commitments for a while, but eventually they'll fall back into their old ways and forget the Ten Commitments ever existed. What would you tell them so they don't give up?"

The Almighty Coach: "Bob, remember when you were nine and you wanted a bicycle so badly that you couldn't stop thinking about it? You kept reminding your parents until they finally bought you one."

Bob: "You knew about that?"

The Almighty Coach: "Sure. I was rooting for you. You wanted that bicycle so badly that I desperately wanted you to get it. It touched me to know that your heart was so full of bicycle longing."

Bob: "What does my bicycle longing have to do with helping people remember the Ten Commitments?"

The Almighty Coach: "They need to want happiness as badly as you wanted that bicycle. Their hearts have to be full of happiness longing."

Bob: "So we need to have a passion for achieving happiness, is that it?"

The Almighty Coach: "Wanting it badly keeps people

working for it, but I hope they don't get too weird about it."

Bob: "What do you mean?"

The Almighty Coach: "I mean be too strict and intense about it when being flexible and having a bit of fun along the way would work better."

Bob: "You're saying to keep our desire for happiness alive, work hard to achieve it, but not so hard that we make ourselves miserable in the process. Am I getting this right?"

The Almighty Coach: "You've got the spirit of it."

Bob: "Is there anything else I should tell people?"

The Almighty Coach: "Tell them I'm rooting for them."

With that, a bolt of lightning exploded overhead and the Almighty Coach vanished into a cloud of swirling colors.

THE ALMIGHTY COACH'S TEN COMMITMENTS

I
Quit beating yourself up with
negative thoughts and stories.
Make up positive ones.

II
Quit envying others.
Appreciate what you have.

III
Quit working so hard to prove yourself.
Accept and like yourself as you are.

IV
Quit being stupid by resisting what you can't change.
Be smart and accept it.

V
Quit getting lost in self-pity.
Do something for others who
have bigger problems than you.

VI
Quit treating yourself and others badly.
Treat yourself and others well.

VII
Quit whining about being unhappy.
To be happy, create a positive attitude.

VIII
Quit making your problems so big.
Notice how small they really are.

IX
Quit being so one-sided.
Create more balance within yourself.

X
Quit thinking your exaggerated fears are true.
Shrink them down to fit in the palm of your hand.

ABOUT THE AUTHOR

Jim Downton received his Ph.D. from the University of California at Berkeley. He taught four years at California State University in San Francisco and thirty-five years at the University of Colorado in Boulder. His research focused on social change and collective dynamics. In addition to publishing articles, he produced three books: *The Persistent Activist: How Peace Commitment Develops and Survives*, (with Paul Wehr), Perseus Press, 1997; *Sacred Journeys: The Conversion of Young Americans to Divine Light Mission*, Columbia University Press, 1979; and *Rebel Leadership: Commitment and Charisma in the Revolutionary Process*, The Free Press, 1973.

At the University of Colorado, Jim taught courses in sociology, including personal development and creativity. His innovative approaches to teaching earned him three of the university's top teaching excellence awards: "The Best Should Teach Award" from the Graduate Teacher Program in 2004, "The Boulder Faculty Assembly Teaching Excellence Award" in

1992, and "The Student/Alumni Teaching Excellence Award" in 1991. For his research, teaching, and service, Jim was promoted to the rank of Full Professor. He retired from the university in 2004.

Jim's teaching inspired him to create the "Life Gardening Project," an effort to help people improve their lives. As part of this project, he leads workshops covering the issues of happiness, personal growth, and creativity, gives public talks, and publishes self-help books. *Why am I so DAMN Unhappy?* is part of this life gardening work, along with four self-help books published by Humanics Publishing Group.

> *Blooming: Teachings of a Woo Master* **(2005)**
> *The Woo Way: A New Way of Living and Being* **(2003)**
> *Playful Mind: Bringing Creativity to Life* **(2003)**
> *Awakening Minds: The Power of Creativity in Teaching* **(2003)**

Jim has been happily married to Mary for forty-six years and they have two daughters. He leads an active life, playing tennis and squash, hiking in the mountains, and creating art in his studio. To learn more about his creative work, visit his website, www.lifegardening.com.

ROBERT D. REED PUBLISHERS ORDER FORM

WITHDRAWN

Call in your order for fast service and quantity discounts!
(541) 347- 9882

OR order on-line at www.rdrpublishers.com using PayPal.
OR order by mail: Make a copy of this form; enclose payment information:
Robert D. Reed Publishers
1380 Face Rock Drive, Bandon, OR 97411

Note: Shipping is $3.50 1st book + $1 for each additional book.

Send indicated books to:
Name: _____
Address: _____
City: _____ State: _____ Zip: _____
Phone: _____ Fax: _____ Cell: _____
E-Mail: _____
Payment by check ☐ or credit card ☐ (*All major credit cards are accepted*)
Name on card: _____
Card Number: _____
Exp. Date: _____ Last 3-Digit number on back of card: _____
Quantity: _____ Total Amount: _____

Why Am I So DAMN Unhappy? And What To Do About It
by James Downton Jr., Ph.D...$11.95 _____

100 Ways to Create Wealth
by Steve Chandler & Sam Beckford .... $24.95 _____

**Housecalls: How We Can All Heal the World
One Visit at a Time**
by Patch Adams, M.D..$11.95 _____

**The Secret of Transitions: How to Move Effortlessly to
Higher Levels of Success**
by Jim Manton .... $14.95 _____

Listening With Heart
by Elizabeth Diane and Andrew Marshall............................$14.95 _____

All You Need is H A R T! Create Love, Joy, and Abundance NOW!
by Helene Rothschild, MS, MA, MFT................................... $14.95 _____

Other book title(s) from website:
_____ $ _____
_____   _____